OXFORD READINGS IN POLITICS
AND GOVERNMENT

MINISTERIAL RESPONSIBILITY

OXFORD READINGS IN POLITICS
AND GOVERNMENT

General Editors: Vernon Bogdanor and Geoffrey Marshall

The readings in this series are chosen from a variety of journals and sources to cover major areas or issues in the study of politics, government, and political theory. Each volume contains an introductory essay by the editor and a select guide to further reading.

MINISTERIAL RESPONSIBILITY

EDITED BY
GEOFFREY MARSHALL

OXFORD UNIVERSITY PRESS

1989

Oxford University Press, Walton Street, Oxford OX2 6DP

Oxford New York Toronto
Delhi Bombay Calcutta Madras Karachi
Petaling Jaya Singapore Hong Kong Tokyo
Nairobi Dar es Salaam Cape Town
Melbourne Auckland
and associated companies in
Berlin Ibadan

Oxford is a trade mark of Oxford University Press

Published in the United States
by Oxford University Press (USA)

Introduction and compilation © Geoffrey Marshall 1989

British Library Cataloguing in Publication Data
Ministerial responsibility.—(Oxford
readings in politics and government).
1. Great Britain. Government. Ministers.
Responsibility
I. Marshall, Geoffrey, 1929–
354.41'04
ISBN 0–19–827580–3
ISBN 0–19–827579–x (pbk.)

Library of Congress Cataloging-in-Publication Data
Ministerial responsibility.
(Oxford readings in politics and government)
Bibliography: p.
1. Ministerial responsibility—Great Britain.
I. Marshall, Geoffrey. II. Series.
JN406.M56 1989 354.4104 88–28880
ISBN 0–19–827580–3
ISBN 0–19–827579–x (pbk.)

Printed in Great Britain
at the University Printing House, Oxford
by David Stanford
Printer to the University

CONTENTS

PART III
INDIVIDUAL RESPONSIBILITY

INTRODUCTION
GEOFFREY MARSHALL

The doctrine of ministerial responsibility is the most general principle of the system of parliamentary government. It is not a single doctrine or rule but a rather complicated bundle of distinct though related principles. Students when asked to define and explain its operation in Britain tend to focus excessively on the notion of ministerial unanimity in speaking and voting. But that is to mistake the principle for one of its parts.

In the first and basic sense ministerial responsibility stands for the system of government that contrasts with the separation of powers as exemplified by its American model. In that system the executive and legislative branches are separately elected for fixed terms as autonomous bodies each deriving its power independently, neither subordinate to the other and each irremovable by the other. A 'responsible' executive is legally and constitutionally non-autonomous, removable and answerable to the legislative branch and in theory thereby to the electorate. In practice the degree to which the constitutionally superior legislative branch can enforce its authority has depended in different parliamentary systems—and in the same parliamentary system at different times—on the structure and organization of political parties.

The idea of responsibility has, in addition to the sense of constitutional subordination, a number of other distinct senses and aspects. There is legal and political and moral responsibility. There is responsibility attributed to governments collectively and to Ministers individually. In either case the forms or modes of operation of the doctrine may vary. Detailed and sometimes controversial rules and conventions of behaviour may develop.

The readings in this volume have been arranged so far as possible to distinguish and illustrate the various types and categories of responsibility.

LEGAL RESPONSIBILITY

In the *Introduction to the Study of the Law of the Constitution* in 1885 Dicey noted that the responsibility of Ministers 'means where used in its strict sense the legal responsibility of every Minister for every act of the Crown in which he takes part'. That sense of individual ministerial responsibility of course still exists and, since 'court proceedings may be brought under the Crown Proceedings Act which were not possible in Dicey's day, it is a form of accountability that is in practice relatively more efficacious. The legal liability of government is a large and complex topic and we are here primarily concerned with political and constitutional accountability, but it is worth noting that it was the decline of the traditional legal sanction of impeachment as a form of individual accountability that is said to have promoted the notion of the Ministry as a unit accepting joint responsibility for each other's actions. Sir William Anson noted that 'since loss of office and of public esteem is the only penalty which Members pay for political failure we can insist that the action of the Cabinet is the action of each member—and that for the actions of each member the Cabinet is responsible as a whole'. But, he added, a member 'may save his colleagues by resignation of office'.[1]

COLLECTIVE RESPONSIBILITY

Collective political responsibility in England stemmed from the single party Cabinet system. That development was not inevitable or inherent in a parliamentary system as such. A different party structure or a series of coalition governments might have developed laxer rules. Indeed, a collective executive body is not the only possible arrangement for a system in which executive power has passed out of the hands of the Crown. 'The substitute for an irremovable and impeccable King might have been a single Grand Vizier or Parliamentary Mayor of the Palace.'[2] But that did not come about. In consequence, the phrase collective responsibility

---

[1] Sir W. Anson, *The Law and Custom of the Constitution* (4th edn., 1935), vol. ii, pt. 2, p. 119.
[2] Sir M. Amos, *The English Constitution* (1930), p. 64.

invokes in the first place the idea that the Crown is advised by, and its powers are in practice exercised by, a collectivity. Despite the theorizing in recent years about the supersession of collective by Prime Ministerial government, the collectivity of executive power is rooted in our constitutional arrangements.

Collective responsibility is generally represented as one of the major conventions of the constitution. It involves however three sets of practices that need separate consideration. They may be called for convenience the Confidence principle, the Unanimity principle, and the Confidentiality principle.

The Confidence principle requires careful stating and is now generally phrased more narrowly than it would have been ten or fifteen years ago. Possibly as the result of smaller parliamentary majorities and disturbances in internal party discipline, defeats, even serious defeats, in the House of Commons are not now thought to entail the constitutional consequences that were once thought inevitable. Only defeats on specific motions of no confidence are now thought to compel governments to resign or advise dissolution. (What counts as a confidence motion is explained in the article by Philip Norton.)

The Unanimity principle—that all members of the administration speak and vote together in the House of Commons—is also subject to a number of queries and qualifications. (See the articles by David Ellis and Arthur Silkin.) To whom does the obligation of solidarity extend and in what contexts? In what sense can the rule or convention be suspended? What are the implications of the suspension of the solidarity rule by the 1932 coalition Government and by the Labour Administration in 1975?

The Confidentiality principle, whether it deserves the name of constitutional convention or not, has been closely if now more controversially associated with the unanimity rules. Unanimity is of necessity a constitutional fiction to which the confidentiality of the Cabinet and of intragovernmental proceedings is an obvious adjunct. That is, up to a point, conceded, but the limits of the principle are not. Both Labour and Conservative Cabinets have resorted to the courts to protect the principle of confidentiality between Ministers, between Ministers and civil servants, and between one government servant and another. Those who oppose excessive security in executive government have urged that members have misused the confidence principle to overprotect procedures and machinery of decision-making from parliamentary and public scrutiny. Collective responsibility, for example, was invoked by Prime Minister James Callaghan as a reason for not disclosing the existence of Cabinet committees. It has consistently been pleaded also as the ground for restricting the contents of ministerial memoirs and the information that can be given by civil servants to Parliamentary Select Committees or to successive political administrations. (See the article by Lord Hunt.) It looks as if the boundary between collective confidentiality (or ministerial prerogative) and openness in government (or non-ministerial inquisitiveness) is going to be a continuously disputed area.

INDIVIDUAL RESPONSIBILITY

Whether and in what sense Ministers are individually responsible to Parliament has been a matter of controversy. In the early years of the century it had become customary to play down the significance of the principle of ministerial responsibility. 'We like to think', said Sidney Low in 1904, '. . . that we can always hang a minister . . . and we feel a kind of pity for peoples who have nobody to hang.' In America, he added, 'you could not think of hanging a minister becuse the minister is only a kind of clerk to the President'.[3] But this apparently formidable principle he thought had become ineffective. The process of proceeding against a particular Minister in the Commons had gone out of fashion. Collective liability would protect a Minister against an adverse vote. Lawrence Lowell's view of individual responsibility in *The Government of England* at about the same time was that 'the joint responsibility has become greater and the several responsibility less'.[4] The last instances in which a single Minister had resigned on an adverse vote of the House of Commons had been Mr Lowe after a vote in 1864 charging him with improper mutilation

[3] S. Low, *The Governance of England* (rev. edn., 1914), p. 138.
[4] A. L. Lowell, *The Government of England*, i (rev. edn., 1919), 73.

of the reports of school inspectors, and Lord Chancellor Westbury in 1866 on account of a vote censuring his grant of a pension to an official charged with misconduct. It was not denied however that in a clear case of personal error on the part of an individual Minister he might be brought to resign without a vote in the House and that some motions in the House though not phrased explicitly as votes of censure on an individual might be taken as critical of a Minister's policy. In 1956 Professor S. E. Finer in an article on 'The Individual Responsibility of Ministers' reached an equally sceptical conclusion. If a Minister's party were out for blood and his Prime Minister unwilling to support him then, however serious or trivial the reason, a Minister might find himself without parliamentary support and forced to resign. That had happened in effect to Sir Thomas Dugdale after the Crichel Down Inquiry into the operations of the Ministry of Agriculture and the Crown Lands Commission in 1954. But an examination of ministerial resignations in the twentieth century indicated no succession of clear cases on which to found a convention about individual answerability of ministers to the Commons in the resigning sense. Ministers were answerable in that they had to explain their conduct. But however badly they behaved, House of Commons censure had not in the face of party solidarity produced an effective sanction against individual ministerial wrongdoing.

Perhaps we are faced here with some uncertainty about whether we are looking for evidence of an effective working principle of individual accountability. If that is the object of the sanction, then clearly it would make sense to say that there is no such effective working convention of individual ministerial responsibility. It would be equally true to say that House of Commons censure of governments collectively is not an effective sanction for collective efficiency or propriety, given the dominance of party majorities in the twentieth century. But is the existence of a rule or convention of constitutional behaviour entirely determined by evidence of this kind? The collective convention is not normally stated as a proposition that governments will be defeated by withdrawal of the House's confidence if they act in such a way as to merit defeat, but in the form of a rule or rules stating the entitlement of the

House to pass motions of no confidence, and a consequent political or constitutional obligation on the part of a government to resign or dissolve in consequence. There seems no doubt that the Commons is entitled to censure a particular Minister. If a Minister's colleagues allowed or were unable to prevent such a vote from being carried, there is some evidence that an expectation exists that a Minister finding himself in that situation ought to offer his resignation and his ministerial colleagues ought to accept it. They would clearly not be obliged to treat defeat on such a motion as a vote of no confidence in the government (though they might do so if they wished). In practice the individual responsibility convention has been related not merely to censure votes in the House but to the wider proposition that a Minister should offer resignation if guilty of either significant personal or political misjudgement. Whether a government as a whole has been guilty of such error can only be established in effect by the judgement of the Commons and the electorate. But there are other forms of evidence that may establish individual ministerial transgression—for example the results of a tribunal or court hearing, or investigations by the Press or broadcasting media.

At the time of Professor Finer's article the resignation of Sir Thomas Dugdale which followed criticism of his department in the report of a public inquiry was perhaps the only example since the First World War of a ministerial resignation following upon political or administrative misjudgement. But there have been a number of examples of ministerial resignation as the result of personal moral or financial misdemeanours not connected with the work of their departments. Since the Second World War more than forty Ministers have resigned their offices. The majority of them have been on the face of it examples of Ministers voluntarily withdrawing from a government on policy grounds (in the manner required by the unanimity rule of the collective responsibility convention). A smaller number have been 'forced' resignations that may be related to the convention of personal and political responsibility, and of this number perhaps three or four are clear cases of Ministers resigning on political grounds in apparent deference to the individual responsibility convention.

MINISTERS AND CIVIL SERVANTS

The major element of uncertainty in the doctrine of individual ministerial responsibility for the actions of officials concerns its application to the duty of resignation for administrative mismanagement. Nobody doubts that Ministers should resign if they sell secrets to the enemy or have mistresses who write rude letters about them to *The Times* or if they tell lies to the House of Commons (except on matters of major policy). But the extent to which they have an obligation to resign in expiation of administrative error or negligence in which they have had no personal hand or direct influence has been a matter of dispute.

RESPONSIBILITY FOR DEPARTMENTAL ACTION: LAW AND CONVENTION CONFUSED?

It is not easy to find in the textbooks a straightforward official statement of the doctrine of pure vicarious ministerial liability sanctioned by the Minister's resignation. But many accounts, like Lowell's, sound as if they carry that strong implication. 'The Minister', Lowell wrote (in 1908), 'is alone responsible for everything done in his department.'[5] Sir Ivor Jennings had a similar view: 'The act of every civil servant is by convention regarded as the act of his minister.'[6] Lord Morrison in the 1950s said that 'the Minister is responsible for every stamp stuck on an envelope'.[7] In *Government and Parliament* he wrote that 'If a mistake is made in a Government Department the Minister is responsible even if he knew nothing about it' and 'publicly he must accept responsibility as if the act were his own'.[8] But these remarks may be misleading. In one sense Lowell's and Morrison's statements are correct. They were stating the formal implication of the proposition set out by Dicey in 1885 in his *Law of the Constitution*. As a maxim of constitutional law the responsibility of Ministers means that some person is legally responsible for every act done by the

---

[5] Lowell, op. cit., p. 192.
[6] Sir I. Jennings, *The Law and the Constitution* (5th edn., 1959), p. 208.
[7] Speaking in the Crichel Down debate. 530 HC Deb. 5s. col. 1278 (1954).
[8] Lord Morrison, *Government and Parliament* (3rd edn., 1964), p. 329.

Crown. This followed, he said, from several principles: first, the King could do no wrong; secondly, 'the minister who affixes a particular seal or counter-signs his signature is responsible for the act which he, so to speak, endorses'.[9] In addition, what is true of prerogative acts is also true of statutory powers. Where not conferred on Her Majesty-in-Council they are vested in a Minister, and when that is so, legal responsibility and liability to suit for all official exercises of these powers rests formally on him. Lowell echoes something of this. 'The permanent official', he says, 'like the King can do no wrong.' But both he and Sir Ivor Jennings risk an illegitimate conclusion by not sufficiently distinguishing the legal and the conventional rules. Dicey's legal proposition is that acts done by civil servants generally speaking are treated for legal purposes as acts of the Minister. But it does not by any means follow from that that every civil servant's act is by *convention* the act of his Minister. If it did, then moral and political culpability, and in appropriate cases, resignation, for political error would certainly follow. But it is not so, and if it were so it would at least have to be for some other reason. Two contributory propositions—one true, the other dubious—may have compounded the confusion between the legal and conventional senses of responsibility and helped to support the growth of an erroneous doctrine. The first is that Parliament acts through ministers and has no direct constitutional linkage with the Civil Service. It cannot itself punish or dismiss civil servants. Consequently discipline or control must be exercised by the Minister. The second principle is also often asserted but is not entailed by any of the other principles—namely (in Lowell's words) that the Minister 'receives all the credit and all the blame . . . and on the other hand the minister ought not to attribute blunders or misconduct to a subordinate, unless prepared at the same time to announce his discharge'.[10] Lowell admitted that this rule was not always observed. In 1901 'the First Lord of the Admiralty in the House of Lords laid the blame for the capsizing of the

---

[9] *Introduction to the Study of the Law of the Constitution* (10th edn., ed. E. C. S. Wade), p. 25.
[10] Lowell, op. cit., p. 192.

royal yacht at her launching upon the naval constructor while praising at the same time his skill in designing battleships'.[11]

BLAMING AND NAMING

So uncertainty about the conventional rule and the degree to which there existed an obligation to shoulder culpability and with it an implied duty of resignation continued to plague the textbooks and to cloud the issue of political accountability. Matters were not much improved by the debate over the resignation of Sir Thomas Dugdale in the Crichel Down affair in 1954, possibly because it was not clear at the time why the Minister of Agriculture was resigning. Many saw it then as a case of a good Minister sacrificing himself for misbehaving civil servants. But to many of his own supporters the policy he had pursued was not that of a sound Minister and there is something to be said for the view that the civil servants were forced into positions of difficulty by switches in policy and indecision at the political level.[12] So possibly good civil servants were sacrificed unfairly for misbehaving Ministers rather than vice versa. In the Commons debate there was some philosophizing about ministerial responsibility and the then Home Secretary, Sir David Maxwell Fyfe, said that where official mistakes have been made that are not on an important issue of policy or where a claim to undoubted rights is involved and if the Minister has been unaware of the action and not personally involved, he 'accepts the responsibility', protecting the civil servant from criticism and stating that he will take corrective action. Presumably he also accepts the responsibility if important matters or undoubted rights *are* involved. And presumably in that case also he orders corrective action. It was not clear whether Sir David Maxwell Fyfe intended to draw any significant distinction between the two cases or between accepting responsibility in the one case and accepting it in the other.[13] Both the Home Secretary and

---

[11] Ibid.

[12] A thesis urged in I. F. Nicolson, *The Mystery of Crichel Down* (1986).

[13] The responsibility for initiating corrective action has been dubbed by Colin Turpin 'amendatory responsibility' (see his 'Ministerial Responsibility: Myth or Reality?' in J. Jowell and D. Oliver (edd.), *The Changing Constitution* (Oxford, 1985)).

Mr Herbert Morrison, though, were prepared to say—as Lowell forty odd years earlier had not been—that public blaming of civil servants was permitted. 'A minister', Maxwell Fyfe said, 'is not bound to approve of action of which he did not know or of which he disapproves.' This is not the clearest of sentences. It would be very odd if a Minister was bound to approve of action of which he disapproved. But what it comes down to is that he can say out loud that he did not know, and say whose conduct it is that he is not bound to approve of when he disapproves of it. 'It is quite untrue', Maxwell Fyfe went on, 'that well justified public criticism of the actions of civil servants cannot be made on a suitable occasion.'[14] So civil servants are not anonymous and can in justified cases be blamed and named. If it is permissible only in justified cases, that seems to be satisfactory. In fact after the Crichel Down inquiry and debate five individual officers were named in the report of a committee set up by the Prime Minister to consider whether they should be transferred to other duties[15] and one of them, the Permanent Commissioner of Crown Lands, was transferred. Various inquisitory procedures have also been initiated by legislation that may result in the fixing of blame on individual civil servants. One is the Tribunals of Inquiry (Evidence) Act procedure dating from 1921. In 1972 a tribunal under the Act appointed to examine the Department of Trade and Industry's responsibility for the collapse of the Vehicle and General Insurance Company concluded that a named Under-Secretary and two named assistant secretaries were responsible for the Department's failure to act that constituted negligence.[16] Reports by the Parliamentary Commissioner for Administration may have the same result. The logic of this is that when the House of Commons Select Committee on the Parliamentary Commissioner follows up the Commissioner's reports they may, if he has placed the blame for maladministration on particular civil servants, wish to pursue the matter and even possibly cross-examine the civil

It might be useful to distinguish resigning, responding to questions, and correcting error as 'sacrificial', 'explanatory', and 'amendatory' responsibility.

[14] 530 HC Deb. 5s cols. 1289–90.
[15] Cmd. 9220 (1954).
[16] HC 133 (1971–2).

servants in question as to their own actions, perhaps to determine how far they were acting under instructions. The PCA Committee tried to do that in the Sachsenhausen case in 1968 when the Foreign Office civil servants were held to have caused injustice by reason of maladministration. The Defence Committee tried to do it in 1986 when they were investigating the leaking of the Solicitor-General's letter to Mr Heseltine and the Government's decision-making in the Westland Helicopter controversy. In both cases the Government prevented the civil servants from appearing, thus provoking a clash, as yet unresolved, between two theories of ministerial accountability, one held in Whitehall and the other at Westminster. The Westminster theory must be that if it is legitimate to identify and publicize maladministration in government it is legitimate to find out who caused it and through what precise blend of ministerial and official misjudgement it came about. It is implied that all parliamentary scrutiny committees are entitled to concern themselves with and inquire into executive maladministration in the sense that that term is used in the Parliamentary Commissioner legislation of 1967. That includes maladministration by Ministers.

DISTANCING MINISTERS

All of this has certainly conspired to eliminate—if it ever existed—the theory that Ministers are obliged to accept blame or a liability to resign when civil servants are held to have acted wrongly. That is not to say that both may not be blameworthy, but pure vicarious headrolling is not required. In 1984 the serious mismanagement that led to the escape of thirty-eight IRA prisoners from the Maze prison in Northern Ireland was (in Maxwell Fyfe's terminology) an important issue affecting individual rights. The Prison Governor resigned, but the Northern Ireland Secretary Mr James Prior said feelingly (if ungrammatically) 'I do not believe there was negligence by myself'. Consequently neither he himself nor the Junior Minister resigned. This now seems accepted doctrine. As Sir John Hunt phrased it in 1977, 'The concept that because somebody whom the Minister has never heard of has made a mistake means that the Minister should resign is out of date and rightly so.'[17]

The situation of Mr Leon Brittan in 1986 however was rather more mysterious. He had certainly heard of Mr Bernard Ingham and Sir John Mogg and Miss Bowe. But we do not know if his resignation was on the basis of personal fault or Civil Service fault or both. The conviction of innocent disengagement that affected Mr Prior cannot have pulsed quite so strongly in him. But he may well have felt that in engineering the Press leakage of the Solicitor-General's letter to Mr Heseltine, the Prime Minister's officials and his own had carried out his policies in a manner that he would not have approved of if he had known of it in detail. That was Mrs Thatcher's presentation of the matter. Her private office had not told her exactly what they were at with the Solicitor-General's letter and she would not have approved of the way in which it was done. Neither did the civil servants reveal to her, she said, that Mr Brittan's officials had asked her office for authorization to leak the letter and had presumably been asked to do it by Mr Brittan. Nobody told her for sixteen days that it was Mr Brittan and if nobody told her Mr Brittan cannot have told her. Perhaps he thought that she did not need to be told. When the Select Committee asked him if he had told her he would not tell them whether he had told her and when they asked him if he had authorized the leak he would not tell them that either. We know that Mr Brittan's Head of Information Miss Colette Bowe acted under instruction, so somebody in or out of the Home Office originated the policy for which the Home Secretary took responsibility by resignation. But he seems less a Minister placed in embarrassing circumstances by his officials than one left to squirm in them by a senior political colleague. Sir Samuel Hoare may have felt much the same in 1935 about Stanley Baldwin.

ADMINISTRATORS AND MINISTERS:
FURTHER QUESTIONS

Largely because of the travails of Miss Bowe and Clive

[17] See Eleventh Report from the Expenditure Committee (The Civil Service) HC 535-I (1955), p. xlvii.

Ponting and Sarah Tisdall, the nature and limits of the duties that civil servants owe to Ministers were considered in some detail by the Commons Treasury and Civil Service Select Committee in 1985–6. The evidence given to the Committee and the Government's response show that there are now some major issues about the implications of ministers' responsibilities, in relation both to the Commons and to the permanent Civil Service, that at the present time remain unresolved.

PART I

RESPONSIBLE GOVERNMENT
ITS PRINCIPLES

THE PRINCIPLES OF CABINET GOVERNMENT

LORD MORLEY

The founders of the American constitution, as all know, followed Montesquieu's phrases, if not his design, about separating legislature from executive, by excluding Ministers from both Houses of Congress. This is fatal to any reproduction of the English system. The American cabinet is vitally unlike our own on this account. If Walpole had taken the line afterwards adopted at Philadelphia, ministerial responsibility would have borne a very different sense from that with which we are now so familiar, as almost to regard it as of divine ordinance. In no direction did Walpole give a more important turn to our affairs. He imparted a decisive bias at a highly critical moment; though the struggle was a long one, it is to Walpole more especially that we owe it that government in England is carried on, not by royal or imperial ministers, as in Prussia, nor by popular ministers, as in the United States, but by parliamentary Ministers.

The principal features of our system of Cabinet government today are four. The first is the doctrine of collective responsibility. Each Cabinet Minister carries on the work of a particular department, and for that department he is individually answerable. When Pitt's Administration came to an end in 1801, and Lord Loughborough was displaced from the woolsack, the ex-Chancellor, to the amazement of the new Prime Minister, kept the key of the Cabinet boxes, and actually, without being summoned, attended meetings of the Cabinet. At last Addington wrote to beg him to discontinue his attendance, on the principle that 'the number of the Cabinet should not exceed that of the persons whose

From *The Life of Walpole* (1889).

responsible situations in office require their being members of it'. In addition to this individual responsibility each Minister largely shares a collective responsibility with all other members of the Government, for anything of high importance that is done in every other branch of the public business besides his own. The question whether the mistakes or misdeeds of one Minister involves all the rest, is of course not quite independent of the position of the Minister, or of the particular action. The censure and impeachment of Lord Melville, for example, was so purely personal in its bearings that it did not break up the Government of Mr Pitt. But as a general rule every important piece of departmental policy is taken to commit the entire Cabinet, and its members stand or fall together. The Chancellor of the Exchequer may be driven from office by a bad dispatch from the Foreign Office, and an excellent Home Secretary may suffer for the blunders of a stupid Minister of War. The Cabinet is a unit—a unit as regards the sovereign, and a unit as regards the legislature. Its views are laid before the sovereign and before Parliament, as if they were the views of one man. It gives its advice as a single whole, both in the royal closet, and in the hereditary or the representative chamber. If that advice be not taken, provided the matter of it appear to be of proper importance, then the Cabinet, before or after an appeal to the electors, dissolves itself and disappears. The first mark of the Cabinet, as that institution is now understood, is united and indivisible responsibility.

The second mark is that the Cabinet is answerable immediately to the majority of the House of Commons, and ultimately to the electors whose will creates that majority. Responsibility to the Crown is slowly ceasing to be more than a constitutional fiction, though even as a fiction it possesses many practical conveniences. William IV, it is true, dismissed the Melbourne Government in 1834 of his own motion, and Sir Robert Peel stuck to the helm for his hundred days in spite of a hostile majority. But though such experiments may by bare possibility recur, they will hardly recur often, and they will never last long. The only real responsibility is to the House of Commons. Responsibility to the House of Lords means no more than that that House may temporarily resist

Bills of which it disapproves, until the sense of the electors of the House of Commons has been taken upon them. Even in Walpole's time, when the House of Lords passed a motion of censure upon the Spanish Convention in 1739, the Minister paid no attention to it.

Third, the Cabinet is, except under uncommon, peculiar, and transitory circumstances, selected exclusively from one party. There have been coalitions of men of opposite parties, but in most cases, down to the present time, coalition has been only the preliminary of fusion. There have been conjunctions, again, of men openly holding directly opposite opinions on subjects going to the very foundations of government, and turning on the very principles that mark party difference. Lord Liverpool's Ministry, for instance, lasted for fourteen years, with so important an issue as Catholic emancipation left an open question. But notwithstanding both coalitions and open questions, it remains generally true that Cabinets are made from one party.

Fourth, the Prime Minister is the keystone of the Cabinet arch. Although in Cabinet all its members stand on an equal footing, speak with equal voice, and, on the rare occasions when a division is taken, are counted on the fraternal principle of one man, one vote, yet the head of the Cabinet is *primus inter pares*, and occupies a position which, so long as it lasts, is one of exceptional and peculiar authority.

THE HOUSE OF COMMONS AND THE EXECUTIVE

SIDNEY LOW

What has been said of legislation applies largely to administration. The House of Commons no longer controls the Executive; on the contrary, the Executive controls the House of Commons. The theory is that the Ministers must justify each and all of their acts before the representatives of the nation at every stage; if they fail to do so, those representatives will turn them out of office. But in our modern practice the Cabinet is scarcely ever turned out of office by Parliament *whatever it does*. The Ministry may fall by its own connivance as in 1885 and 1895, when it feels that the country is turning against it; or it may break up on some question, like that of Home Rule or Free Trade, upon which its own members are divided. But such a question will be one of policy, not of administrative action. It is very difficult to bring a government to account for anything done in its ministerial work.

The real check upon a too gross and salient misuse of ministerial power is, no doubt, the salutary fear of public opinion; but this is a restraint that would be pretty nearly as operative without the assistance of the House of Commons which does not respond to it except after a general election. For the control of Parliament, which was supposed to be regular, steady, and constant, is exchanged the control of the electorate, which is powerful but intermittent. It is brought into operation at uncertain intervals, and is exercised only with reference to one or two great issues of policy, often determined by Ministers themselves, instead of being applied, from day to day, to the conduct of public affairs. The country may change its politics in consequence of the acts or omissions of the

From *The Governance of England* (1904).

Executive, but the rank and file of the House do not. If they do, we should find members constantly, or at any rate occasionally, voting with the Opposition; but that scarcely ever happens. Even when a party is broken by internal dissension, members are very reluctant to vote *against* the official leaders, though they will sometimes abstain from voting *with* them. This was the case with the Free Trade Unionists in the various debates which arose out of Mr Chamberlain's Preferential agitation. Only a very small knot of the 'free fooders' voted regularly with the Opposition in the Session of 1904, though they were quite as strongly opposed as the Liberals to the fiscal views of the chief members of the Cabinet. The custom of voting with the party has solidified into a rule; and that rule established, the control of Parliament tends to become sensibly attenuated, till for long periods of time it is almost non-existent for practical purposes.

3

MINISTERIAL RESPONSIBILITY
AND THE
RULE OF LAW

A. V. DICEY

Ministerial responsibility means two utterly different things.

It means in ordinary parlance the responsibility of Ministers to Parliament, or, the liability of Ministers to lose their offices if they cannot retain the confidence of the House of Commons.

This is a matter depending on the conventions of the constitution with which law has no direct concern.

It means, when used in its strict sense, the legal responsibility of every Minister for every act of the Crown in which he takes part.

This responsibility, which is a matter of law, rests on the following foundation. There is not to be found in the law of England, as there is found in most foreign constitutions, an explicit statement that the acts of the monarch must always be done through a Minister, and that all orders given by the Crown must, when expressed in writing, as they generally are, be countersigned by a Minister. Practically, however, the rule exists.

In order that an act of the Crown may be recognized as an expression of the Royal will and have any legal effect whatever, it must in general be done with the assent of, or through some Minister or Ministers who will be held responsible for it. For the Royal will can, speaking generally, be expressed only in one of three different ways, viz. (1) by Order in Council; (2) by order, commission, or warrant under the sign-manual; (3) by proclamations, writs, patents, letters, or other documents under the Great Seal.

From *Introduction to the Study of the Law of the Constitution* (10th edn., ed. E. C. S. Wade) (1st edn., 1885).

An Order in Council is made by the Queen 'by and with the advice of her Privy Council'; and those persons who are present at the meeting of the Council at which the order was made, bear the responsibility for what was there done. The sign-manual warrant, or other document to which the sign-manual is affixed, bears in general the countersignature of one responsible Minister or of more than one; though it is not unfrequently authenticated by some one of the seals for the use of which a Secretary of State is responsible. The Great Seal is affixed to a document on the responsibility of the Chancellor, and there may be other persons also, who, as well as the Chancellor, are made responsible for its being affixed. The result is that at least one Minister and often more must take part in, and therefore be responsible for, any act of the Crown which has any legal effect, e.g. the making of a grant, the giving of an order, or the signing of a treaty.

The Minister or servant of the Crown who thus takes part in giving expression to the Royal will is legally responsible for the act in which he is concerned, and he cannot get rid of his liability by pleading that he acted in obedience to royal orders. Now supposing that the act done is illegal, the Minister concerned in it becomes at once liable to criminal or civil proceedings in a court of law. In some instances, it is true, the only legal mode in which his offence could be reached may be an impeachment. But an impeachment itself is a regular though unusual mode of legal procedure before a recognized tribunal, namely, the High Court of Parliament. Impeachments indeed may, though one took place as late as 1805, be thought now obsolete, but the cause why this mode of enforcing ministerial responsibility is almost out of date is partly that Ministers are now rarely in a position where there is even a temptation to commit the sort of crimes for which impeachment is an appropriate remedy, and partly that the result aimed at by impeachment could now in many cases be better obtained by proceedings before an ordinary court. The point, however, which should never be forgotten is this: it is now well-established law that the Crown can act only through Ministers and according to certain prescribed forms which absolutely require the co-operation of some Minister, such as a Secretary of State or the Lord Chancellor, who thereby becomes not only morally but legally responsible for the legality of the act in which he takes part. Hence, indirectly but surely, the action of every servant of the Crown, and therefore in effect of the Crown itself, is brought under the supremacy of the law of the land. Behind parliamentary responsibility lies legal liability, and the acts of Ministers no less than the acts of subordinate officials are made subject to the rule of law.

4

RESPONSIBILITY IN BRITISH POLITICS

A. H. BIRCH

THE PRINCIPLE

We distinguished three usages of the term 'responsible' when applied to groups taking political decisions. It is used to signify that the decision-makers are responsive to public opinion; it is used to signify that their decisions are prudent and mutually consistent; and it is used to signify that they are accountable for their actions to another body, such as Parliament. And while critics commonly assert (or imply) that governments should be responsible in all these senses, it is clear that there is no necessary link between them. Responsiveness and consistency are desirable ends that are wholly compatible only in rare combinations of circumstance. Accountability is not an end in itself so much as a means whereby one or (to some extent) both of the other ends may be secured. The great virtue of ministerial accountability to Parliament, say admirers of the British constitution, is that it gives Ministers enough independence to pursue consistent policies without giving them so much independence that they can safely ignore public opinion.

Ministerial accountability to Parliament has two aspects: the collective responsibility of Ministers for the policies of the Government and their individual responsibility for the work of their departments. Both forms of responsibility are embodied in conventions which cannot be legally enforced. Both conventions were developed during the nineteenth century, and in both cases the practice was established before the doctrine was announced. Thus, the convention of collective responsibility was developed between 1780 and 1832, but the

Abridged from *Representative and Responsible Government*, Chapter 10, pp. 131–6. Reprinted by permission of Unwin Hyman Limited.

concept of 'responsible government' appears not to have been introduced into British political debates until as late as 1829, and then in relation to Canada rather than Britain.

On 14 May of that year E. G. Stanley (later Lord Derby) presented a petition to the House of Commons which had been signed by over 3,000 citizens of Upper Canada and which asked, among other things, for 'a local and responsible ministry—not stating very clearly of what kind'.[1] In the following years the term was used a good deal by the advocates of constitutional reform in British North America, who demanded that the British Government should accept 'the principle of responsible government'. In a dispatch to the new Governor-General of Canada in 1839, Lord John Russell noted that 'it does not appear, indeed, that any very definite meaning is generally agreed upon by those who call themselves the advocates of this principle', and observed that 'its very vagueness is a source of delusion'.[2] However, in the Durham Report, which had been published earlier in the same year, the principle was said to be one of the central features of the British constitution, which the Canadian reformers wished simply to see applied in their own country. Lord Durham's description of the principle of responsible government was as follows.

In England, this principle has so long been considered an indisputable and essential part of our constitution, that it has really hardly ever been found necessary to inquire into the means by which its observance is enforced. When a ministry ceases to command a majority in Parliament on great questions of policy, its doom is immediately sealed; and it would appear to us as strange to attempt, for any time, to carry on a government by means of ministers perpetually in a minority, as it would be to pass laws with a majority of votes against them. The ancient constitutional remedies, by impeachment and a stoppage of supplies, have never, since the reign of William III, been brought into operation for the purpose of removing a ministry. They have never been called for, because in fact, it has been the habit of ministers rather to anticipate the occurrence of an absolutely hostile vote, and to retire, when supported only by a bare and uncertain majority.[3]

---

[1] HC Deb., ser. 3, Vol. 21, col. 1332.
[2] The dispatch is reprinted in F. P. Lucas (ed.), *Lord Durham's Report* (Oxford, 1912), iii. 332–5.   [3] Ibid. ii. 278–9.

This statement is worth quoting in full because it was the first clear assertion of what later became known as the convention of collective responsibility. In giving the impression that this was a long-established principle of the British constitution, Durham (who was a Radical) was rather misleading. In fact it had been established only during the previous three or four decades, and securely and irrevocably established only since the Reform Act of 1832. It has been authoritatively stated that in 1815 'the responsibility of the cabinet as a whole was difficult to establish',[4] and the same writer notes that 'no ministry between 1783 and 1830 resigned as a result of defeat in the House of Commons; no ministry before 1830 ever resigned on a question of legislation or taxation'.[5]

It is true that, very much earlier, Walpole had asserted that the Ministry should be accountable to Parliament. On 1 February 1739 he told the Commons: 'When I speak here as a minister, I speak as possessing my powers from his Majesty, but as being answerable to this House for the exercise of these powers.'[6] And in 1742, when he was defeated in a parliamentary division, he resigned. Nevertheless, the convention of governmental responsibility cannot be dated from this occasion. For the convention to be established, three developments were necessary. These were: first, the effective unity of the Cabinet; second, effective control of the Cabinet by the Prime Minister; and third, the understanding that if the Cabinet were defeated in Parliament on a major issue or a vote of confidence, the Prime Minister would have no choice but to resign or ask for a dissolution. It will be helpful to sketch the history of these developments in a few sentences.

The effective unity of the Cabinet was established in the period between 1780 and 1815. In 1782 there occurred the first example of the collective resignation of a Ministry. When Lord North resigned in anticipation of a certain parliamentary defeat, all his Ministers, with the one exception of the Lord Chancellor, resigned with him. Following this,

---

[1] E. L. Woodward, *The Age of Reform* (Oxford, 1938), p. 23.
[5] Ibid. 23.
[6] Quoted in W. C. Costin and J. S. Watson, *The Law and Working of the Constitution: Documents 1660–1914* (1952), i. 217.

Pitt, during his long term of office from 1783 to 1800, did a great deal to develop the convention that Cabinet Ministers, whatever their private disagreements, should present a united front on major issues of policy. In 1792 Pitt secured the dismissal of the Lord Chancellor, who had criticized the Prime Minister's policies in Parliament. Another date of some significance is 1812, when an attempt to form a government drawn from opposed groups was rejected as 'inconsistent with the prosecution of any uniform and beneficial course of policy'.[7] It is rarely, if ever, possible to give a precise date for the establishment of a convention, but it seems safe to say that Cabinet unity had become the rule by about 1815.

In the middle decades of the century, the collective responsibility of the Cabinet to Parliament became a cardinal feature of British politics. Lord John Russell, who had questioned the meaning of the principle in 1839, accepted its implications without hesitation in 1852 and 1866, in each case resigning immediately his Government was defeated in Parliament. Between 1832 and 1867 no fewer than ten governments were brought to an end by adverse votes in the Commons;[8] in eight cases the Prime Minister resigned and in the other two he secured a dissolution. In these years not a single government lasted the entire life of a Parliament, from one general election to the next.

It is largely on the experience of these years that the doctrine of collective responsibility is based. It began to appear in textbooks in the 1860s and 1870s. Todd devoted a chapter to it in 1867,[9] and in the same year Bagehot made several references to its consequences. The House of Commons, he said, 'is a real choosing body; it elects the people it likes. And it dismisses whom it likes too.'[10] 'The distinguishing quality of Parliamentary government,' he declared, is that the public 'can, through Parliament, turn out an administration which is not doing as it likes, and can put in an administration which will do as it likes.'[11] Five years later

[7] A. Todd, *On Parliamentary Government in England* (2nd edn., 1887), ii. 142.

[8] The dates were as follows: 1841, 1846, 1851, Feb. 1852, Dec. 1852, 1855, 1857, 1858, 1859, 1866.

[9] Todd, op. cit., vol. ii.

[10] W. Bagehot, *The English Constitution* (1867), p. 116.

[11] Ibid. 302.

the doctrine was stated more formally by E. A. Freeman. 'What we understand by the responsibility of ministers', he wrote, 'is that they are liable to have all their public acts discussed in Parliament.' While impeachment had passed, 'the unwritten constitution makes a vote of censure as effectual as an impeachment, and in many cases it makes a mere refusal to pass a ministerial measure as effectual as a vote of censure.'[12] In this unwritten constitution, the Cabinet is 'a collective body bound together by a common responsibility'.[13] In the following decade the doctrine was stated more briefly by A. V. Dicey: 'the cabinet are responsible to Parliament as a body, for the general conduct of affairs'.[14]

[12] E. A. Freeman, *The Growth of the English Constitution* (1st pub. 1872, 3rd edn., 1876), p. 120.
[13] Ibid. 121.
[14] A. V. Dicey, *Law of the Constitution* (8th edn., 1931), p. 416.

PART II

COLLECTIVE RESPONSIBILITY

5

GOVERNMENT DEFEATS IN THE HOUSE OF COMMONS: MYTH AND REALITY

PHILIP NORTON

Recent Government defeats in the House of Commons' division lobbies have raised the question of what (if anything) a government is constitutionally required to do in response to such defeats. One opinion, still current in some quarters, is that a government must respond to a defeat by reversing it (if possible), or else seeking a vote of confidence by resigning. In 1964 Graeme Moodie observed that, except for free votes, 'it is now assumed as a matter of course that any defeat in the House of Commons must be reversed or else lead to the Government's resigning or dissolving Parliament'.[1] Other sources have implied, albeit not always clearly, that the Government should resign or request a dissolution, with no provision for attempting to reverse a defeat. In 1965 Harvey and Bather claimed that 'failure of party members to support Cabinet decisions in the division lobby will lead either to the resignation of the Government or to a dissolution',[2] while more recently, in a Fabian Tract in 1977, Lisanne Radice asserted that, even in committee, 'the fiction is maintained that every vote is a vote of confidence'.[3] Nor is this view a particularly recent one. As early as 1905 Arthur Balfour was observing that it appeared to be assumed in various parts of the House 'that the accepted constitutional principle is that, when a government suffers defeat, either in Supply or on any other subject, the proper course for His Majesty's responsible

---

Abridged from *Public Law* (1978), pp. 360–70. Reprinted by permission of Stevens & Sons Limited.

[1] G. Moodie, *The Government of Great Britain* (1964), p. 100.
[2] J. Harvey and L. Bather, *The British Constitution* (1965), p. 234.
[3] L. Radice, *Reforming the House of Commons*, Fabian Tract 448 (1977), p. 4.

advisers is either to ask His Majesty to relieve them of their office or to ask His Majesty to dissolve Parliament'.[4] A third view is that the Government should resign or dissolve only in consequence of a defeat on an important issue. This view was implicit in a letter to *The Times* in 1971 from Sir Philip de Zulueta, a former private secretary to Prime Minister Macmillan, in which he claimed that a *three-line* whip was 'a formality which warns supporters of an administration that the government will resign if the vote in question goes against them',[5] and was explicitly expressed by the Leader of the Opposition, Mrs Thatcher, in March 1976 following the Government defeat on its 1976 Expenditure White Paper.[6] These views seem to have gained credence due to the popular perception of the high degree of party cohesion in the Commons' division lobbies, following the advent of party government in the latter half of the nineteenth century. Since it was thought that the Government was hardly ever defeated in the lobbies (on issues important or otherwise), there was little to challenge these views, and, indeed, the perceived absence of defeats could be taken to reinforce them.

However, these views may be described as constitutional myths. They have no basis in fact, nor in any authoritative original source, and are belied by the experience of both the nineteenth and twentieth centuries. Government defeats in the nineteenth century were not uncommon, as the figures given by Lawrence Lowell for the sessions 1847 to 1905 clearly demonstrate: in that period, there were no less than 301 Government defeats in the lobbies on whipped votes.[7] Nor are defeats unknown in the twentieth century, including defeats on important issues. Between February 1905 and February 1978 inclusively, there were *at least* 84 Government defeats in the lobbies on whipped votes, and, of these 50 took place in

[4] HC Deb., CL. col. 49.
[5] *The Times*, 13 July 1971.
[6] Mrs Thatcher contended that defeats on clauses or orders were not resigning matters, but 'when there is a defeat on a matter of major economic strategy, a matter central to the historic nature of the power of the House of Commons over the Executive, that is a resigning matter'. HC Deb., Vol. 907, cols. 642–3. (But see also Mrs Thatcher's comments of the previous evening when she appeared to concede that the Government had the alternative choice of seeking a vote of confidence. HC Deb., Vol. 907, col. 565).
[7] A. L. Lowell, *The Government of England*, ii. (1924), 79–80.

the period after April 1972.[8] The defeats were across the board
in terms of the divisions involved: 48 were on amendments
to legislation, 13 on declaratory or adjournment motions, 6
on Supply votes (or connected procedural motions), 4 on
declared votes of confidence (covering only two occasions,
each of which involved two divisions), 4 on Prayers, 4 on
procedural motions (including a guillotine motion), 3 on the
second or third reading of Bills, and 2 on Ways and Means
resolutions. In only a minority of cases did the Government
seek to reverse the defeat, seek a vote of confidence, or resign.
On only two occasions—both in response to defeats on
declared votes of confidence—did it resign (both occasions
being in 1924), and on only three occasions do defeats appear
to have been followed by confidence motions (at least one of
these being tabled by the Opposition). In the majority of cases
the Government responded in a positive manner to the
majority's wishes, either accepting the defeat outright or in
modified form. In less than a quarter of cases does it appear to
have given a totally negative response, either deliberately
ignoring the defeat or successfully obtaining its reversal at
some later stage. The only change that appears noticeable
during the course of this century is that the House now rarely
bothers to adjourn following a government defeat (which was
once the custom, though not apparently the rule[9]), and
indeed, on occasion, does not even discuss the intentions of the
Government following a defeat, preferring instead to continue
immediately with remaining business.[10] The popular views of
the Government's required response to defeats in the lobbies
rest upon no continuous basis of practice, and hence, in this
sense, may be described as myths.

What then are the constitutional requirements or guidelines
to be followed by a government in the event of a defeat in a

---

[8] The figure of 84 defeats is a minimum one, based upon research of secondary
sources and, selectively, of *Hansard*. The number of defeats listed include figures for
multiple defeats on one issue (e.g. one division to carry an amendment, followed by a
second to carry the amended motion, counts as two defeats).

[9] See the discussion consequent to the defeat of 19 July 1921, HC Deb., Vol. 144,
cols. 2125–8.

[10] See e.g. HC Deb., Vol. 176, cols. 1017–22, and the defeats of July 1974, HC
Deb., Vol. 877, cols. 323, 355, 385, 403, 823, 831; HC Deb., Vol. 878, cols. 513, 525,
529, 543, 551.

whipped division? On what occasions might or should the Government consider resigning, seek a vote of confidence, or merely take a defeat in its stride, accepting or attempting to reverse it as it sees fit? An analysis of defeats suggests that there are essentially three types of defeats, each of which invites a different response from the Government. These three categories of defeat we first briefly outlined in an article in *The Parliamentarian* in July 1976,[11] though further research reveals that they were previously identified in broad terms by Prime Minister Stanley Baldwin in the House of Commons in April 1936.[12]

TYPES OF DEFEAT

The three types of government defeats to take place in whipped divisions may be identified as follows:

1. *Defeats on votes of confidence*

A government defeated on a vote of confidence is expected to resign or request a dissolution. The precedent was established in 1841,[13] and has been maintained since, as, for example, in the nineteenth century, in 1886, 1892, and 1895. In the twentieth century, the Baldwin Government was defeated in two divisions of confidence on 21 January 1924, upon meeting the new Parliament, and consequently resigned. On 8 October 1924 the MacDonald Government was similarly defeated in two divisions of confidence, and consequently requested a dissolution.[14] Only one government has been defeated (in 1979) on a vote of confidence since that occasion.

Votes of confidence may themselves be further subdivided into three distinct categories:

(*a*) *Explicitly worded votes of confidence.* These clearly state that the House has, or has not, confidence in Her Majesty's Government, and debate on them thus centres upon the issue

---

[11] P. Norton, 'The Government Defeat: March 10, 1976', *The Parliamentarian*, 57 (1976), 174–5.
[12] HC Deb., Vol. 310, col. 2445.
[13] See Harvey and Bather, op. cit., pp. 233–4.
[14] HC Deb., Vol. 169, cols. 673–8, 679–86; HC Deb., Vol. 177, cols. 693–704.

of confidence. Governments may occasionally seek explicit votes of confidence, but such motions are more usually tabled by the Opposition employing the negative wording, i.e. 'That this House has no confidence in Her Majesty's Government.' By established convention, the Government permits a debate on them as soon as possible.[15] Although the relatively new Supply procedure, under which the Opposition can move several motions critical of various aspects of Government policy, appears to have led to a reduction in the number of such censure motions,[16] they are still not unknown. The Opposition tabled a motion of no confidence in June 1976,[17] and another in March 1977 following the refusal of the Government to contest the division at the end of the debate on its 1977 Expenditure White Paper.[18]

The carrying of an explicitly worded censure motion against the Government may be regarded as the most effective of the three types of confidence votes. The passage of such a motion puts it beyond doubt that the Government has lost the confidence of the House—there are no other issues to cloud the position—and that its resignation is required. Had Mr Callaghan lost the censure vote in March 1977, as it appeared he might at one stage, he would have been required to go to the Palace.

(b) *Motions made votes of confidence by the declaration of the Government.* The Government, usually at the instigation of the Prime Minister, may decide that a particular issue to be divided upon is so central to its policy that there would be little point in continuing in office if defeated upon it. It therefore conveys to the House its decision to make the vote one of confidence; that is, if defeated upon that issue, it will resign or seek a dissolution. Thus, Mr Heath made the second reading of the 1972 European Communities Bill a vote of confidence, informing the House that 'if this House will not agree to the Second Reading of the Bill . . . my colleagues and I are unanimous that in these circumstances this Parliament cannot sensibly continue'.[19] The Government may also, at its

---

[15] Sir D. Lidderdale (ed.), *Erskine May's Treatise on the Law, Privileges, Proceedings and Usage of Parliament* (19th edn., 1976), p. 283.
[16] Ibid.   [17] HC Deb., Vol. 912, cols. 1446–566.
[18] HC Deb., Vol. 928, cols. 1285–412.   [19] HC Deb., Vol. 831, col. 752.

discretion, declare votes of confidence upon issues which many do not regard as central to its policy. For example, in 1902 a division on the subject of an agreement entered into by the Post Office with the National Telephone Company was made a vote of confidence by the Government,[20] as in 1944 was the division to reverse the defeat suffered on an amendment to the Education Bill.[21] The issue which the MacDonald Government made one of confidence in 1924— the Liberal amendment calling for an inquiry into the Campbell case—and upon which it lost, precipitating a dissolution, was also one which many considered hardly central to Government policy or its ability to continue in office. The reason for such action by the Government will often be the desire to avoid defeat through appealing to party loyalty to override objections to the Government line involved, though, as in MacDonald's case in 1924, there are exceptions.

Votes of confidence falling in this category are somewhat less straightforward than those in the previous category, since they are complicated by the debate upon the issue which has been made one of confidence. Governments may also try to hedge their bets by conveying the impression to their supporters that they regard a particular division as one involving confidence without making that fact explicit. Hence Government supporters are subjected to the pull of party loyalty, while the Government has avoided formally committing itself to resignation in the event of a defeat in the lobbies.

(c) *Implicit votes of confidence.* A very small number of issues— indeed, essentially only one—are taken to be confidence votes even though not explicitly worded as such and without the Government having declared them to be so. The granting of Supply is the issue primarily involved here. Failure to grant Supply is regarded as the traditional means by which the House can demonstrate its lack of confidence in Her Majesty's Government. Without the granting of Supply, the Government cannot carry on 'the essential business of governing'.[22] In

---

[20] S. Low, *The Governance of England* (1904), pp. 146–7.

[21] See HC Deb., Vol. 398, col. 1452; and Thelma Cazalet-Keir, *From the Wings* (1967), pp. 143–5.

[22] Ronald Butt, *The Times*, 24 Feb. 1977.

practice, though, failure to grant Supply as a means of expressing lack of confidence in a Ministry would today prove a difficult and complex task. A defeat on a specific estimate would not in itself constitute a vote of no confidence—Balfour refused to treat such a defeat as a censure vote in 1905[23]—nor would a defeat on one of the motions now possible under Supply procedure to reduce a Minister's salary by a nominal amount. When the Government was defeated on such a motion in February 1976, it successfully sought its reversal six days later.[24] Given the number of divisions which annually occur on items of Supply, and the fact that second reading debates on Consolidated Fund Bills are now recognized as private members' time, the ability of the House to declare its lack of confidence in the Government through debating and then refusing Supply *in one division* hardly exists; the only division in which it *might* be possible would be on the second reading of the Appropriation Bill. The most effective means whereby the House could declare its lack of confidence would be through an explicitly worded motion of no confidence. If the Government wilfully then refused to resign or go to the country, the House could refuse throughout the session to pass the Consolidated Fund Bill, the Appropriation Bill, and other items of Supply.[25] (In practice, the political situation would likely be such that the Government found itself unable to govern anyway.) Defeat on one important item of Supply— and also on a Finance Bill (which some would include within the category of implicit votes of confidence)—may clearly raise the question of confidence in the Government, but would probably be insufficient in itself to be now regarded as a vote of no confidence.[26]

---

[23] HC Deb., CXLIX, cols. 1485–90; HC Deb., CL, cols. 49–62.

[24] HC Deb., Vol. 905, cols. 521–6, 1199–204. This negates the assertion of O. H. Phillips, *Constitutional and Administrative Law* (5th edn., 1973), p. 187, that such defeats are matters of confidence.

[25] Note the similar comments of I. Jennings, *Cabinet Government* (1936), pp. 367–8.

[26] Similarly, a censure vote on an individual Minister would be insufficient to constitute a vote of no confidence *in the Government*. 'Even in cases when an individual Minister is censured by the House, the Government is not obliged to resign, unless it decides to share his fate.' B. S. Markesinis, *The Theory and Practice of Dissolution of Parliament* (1972), p. 95.

2. Defeats on items central to government policy

If defeated upon an item which is regarded as central to Government policy, but one which has not been made an issue of confidence beforehand, the Government may decide *either* to seek an explicit vote of confidence from the House *or* to resign or request a dissolution. The effect of deciding upon the latter course (resigning or seeking a dissolution) would be to make the division retrospectively one of confidence. Although there were instances of governments pursuing this course in the nineteenth century—as, for example, the minority Derby Government in 1859 following defeat on its Reform Bill, Russell's Government in 1866 following defeat on an amendment to its Representation of the People Bill (though Russell himself would have preferred to seek a vote of confidence from the House[27]), and Gladstone's Ministry in 1885 following the carrying of an amendment to the Budget—no government in the twentieth century has pursued such a course. Pursuing the former course (seeking a vote of confidence from the House) has proved almost as rare in this century. In 1944, the coalition Government sought the reversal of a defeat on an amendment to the Education Bill on a vote of confidence, and in 1976, following defeat on its Public Expenditure proposals (a declaratory motion), the Wilson Government successfully sought a vote of confidence the following evening,[28] although the Leader of the House, Mr Edward Short, had apparently raised in Cabinet the alternative course of seeking a dissolution.[29]

The reason for few defeats falling into this category in this century is because of the nature of the defeats themselves, and because the task of adjudging whether they do constitute defeats on items central to Government policy rests primarily, though not exclusively, with the Government itself. It may utilize this power to resign following defeats on issues which many do not regard as central items which raise questions of confidence (for example, the resignation of the Government in

---

[27] P. Magnus, *Gladstone* (1963), pp. 180–1.
[28] See P. Norton, loc. cit.; HC Deb., Vol. 907, cols. 634–758.
[29] *Daily Express*, 12 Mar. 1976.
[30] The Queen had advised Russell it was his duty to stay in office, and Russell

1866[30]) or to treat as matters of confidence defeats viewed by many as important but not central to Government policy (for example, the amendment to the 1944 Education Bill). Alternatively, it may utilize this power to adjudge that defeats on issues which its opponents may regard as falling within this category do not do so (for example, the defeat of the Rosebery Government on an amendment to the Address in 1894, Balfour's defeat on the estimates in 1905, and Attlee's defeat on adjournment following a debate on fuel and power in 1950[31]). With the possible exception of the MacDonald Government in 1924, governments in the twentieth century have shown a perhaps not unnatural desire to remain in office, and hence have tended to utilize their power to interpret defeats in a way that will not jeopardize their tenure of office.

This power of interpretation is nevertheless not exclusively held by the Government. Although the power to seek a dissolution consequent to a defeat—or for whatever purpose—rests with the Prime Minister, the power to put the Ministry to a vote of confidence in the House is shared with the Opposition. If the Government fails to seek a vote of confidence following defeat on an issue which its opponents regard as central to its policy, the Opposition may itself table a motion of censure. In 1976 the Wilson Government had sought a vote of confidence following its defeat on its 1976 Expenditure White Paper; the following year, the Callaghan Government—featuring a similar defeat—allowed its 1977 White Paper to be debated on an adjournment motion, and then failed to contest the division.[32] The Leader of the Opposition, Mrs Thatcher, responded by tabling a motion of censure. It was in order to survive the vote on this motion that the Government, by that time lacking an overall majority in the House, entered into a pact with the Liberal parliamentary party.

---

himself felt it was not necessary to resign. The Cabinet itself took a week before deciding upon resignation. Magnus, op. cit., pp. 180–1.

[31] The following day, Attlee had advised the House that the Government did not regard the vote as one of confidence, and intended to carry on. HC Deb., Vol. 473, cols. 566–8.

[32] HC Deb., Vol. 928, cols. 763–6. The voting was 293–0.

3. *Defeats on items not considered central to government policy*

If the Government is defeated on an item which is not considered central to its policy, then no question arises of confidence, unless the Government, or Opposition, wishes it to. The Government need neither contemplate nor seek a vote of confidence, let alone consider submitting its resignation. All that such a defeat requires is that the Government consider whether to accept it or seek, if possible, to reverse it at some later stage.

The overwhelming majority of government defeats fall into this category. This is not surprising given the nature of most divisions in the House; only a handful each year are likely to involve clearly the issue of confidence in the Government. The Government may introduce a Bill which is considered central to its policy. The second reading of the Bill may be made one of confidence. Even if it is not, failure to carry it may raise the issue of confidence, that is, put it into the second category identified above. The carrying of an amendment against the Government—unless it is a wrecking amendment or strikes a central provision from the measure—would, by contrast, not involve a question of confidence, and the number of amendments divided upon will, as a rule, obviously exceed the small number of divisions involved on the principle of the Bill on second and third readings. Thus, on the 1972 European Communities Bill, the second reading fell into the category of a Government-declared vote of confidence, while third reading, the 'stand part' division on Clause 2, and (almost certainly) the guillotine motion fell into the second category identified above. There were well over eighty other divisions on the measure, primarily amendments moved by the Opposition or dissident Conservative back-benchers, which, if carried, would have been politically embarrassing for Mr Heath and his colleagues (as well as creating problems for the Government's business managers[33]), but would not have *necessitated* a consequent vote of confidence or the resignation of the Government. As one Conservative dissenter noted, he and his like-minded colleagues did not want to defeat the

---

[33] The Government was resisting all amendments on committee stage (taken on the floor of the House) in order apparently to avoid a report stage.

Government on second reading, knowing that such an action would bring it down, but they would have liked some amendments to have been carried.[34] On less important measures, the Government may even be prepared to regard second or third reading or wrecking amendments as not involving a question of confidence. In 1924, the MacDonald Government lost the second reading of its Rent Restrictions Bill, and in 1977 the Callaghan Government lost both the second reading of its Reduction of Redundancy Rebates Bill and the Third Reading of its Local Authority Works (Scotland) Bill. In none of these cases did the Government seek a vote of confidence. In 1976, the Government was also defeated on the central provision of its Dock Work Regulation Bill; again, no vote of confidence was sought.

Most government defeats in this century have fallen into this category. Most have been on amendments to legislation, and have included amendments to Finance Bills in 1921, 1924, 1965, 1974, and 1975 (all of them accepted by the Government of the day), as well as amendments to other measures in 1919 (Alien Restrictions Bill), 1924 (London Traffic Bill, Unemployment Insurance Bill, Housing [Financial Provisions] Bill), 1931 (Education [School Attendance] Bill, Representation of the People [No. 2] Bill), 1944 (Education Bill), 1951 (Forestry Bill), 1958 (Maintenance Orders Bill), 1972 (Housing Finance Bill, Local Government Bill, Criminal Justice Bill), 1973 (Maplin Development Bill), 1974 (Trade Union and Labour Relations Bill, Health & Safety at Work Etc. Bill), 1975 (Social Security Benefits Bill, Industry Bill, Housing Finance [Special Provisions] Bill, 1976 (Dock Work Regulation Bill), 1977 (Scotland and Wales Bill, Criminal Law Bill, Scotland Bill), and 1978 (Scotland Bill). In the majority of cases, these defeats were accepted by the Government of the day. On only one occasion did the Government treat defeat on an amendment as raising a question of confidence, when the Prime Minister, Winston Churchill, over-reacted to the defeat on the amendment to the Education Bill in 1944. Indeed, the Prime Minister even went as far to declare that, if the Government did not secure an

---

[34] Conservative MP to author.

'adequate' majority in the second division, it would entail the 'usual constitutional consequences',[35] in so doing overlooking the fact that the 'usual' constitutional consequences of a government obtaining a majority in a confidence vote was to continue in office.[36]

Other defeats to fall into this category have included defeats on Prayers to annul orders in 1951 (twice), 1953, and 1972, the most important of these being the last one—on the immigration rules in November 1972—when fifty-six Conservative back-benchers dissented on a three-line whip. The Government, in consequence, introduced a new order acceptable to the dissenters.[37] Other defeats have been on Ways and Means resolutions in 1912 and 1924 (the Asquith Government initially sought to reverse the defeat of 1912, but under pressure from the Opposition and a resignation threat from the Speaker modified its intention[38]); on motions for Mr Speaker to leave the Chair in 1923 and 1936; on various declaratory motions in 1920, 1924, 1973, 1974 (three times), 1976 (twice, to reduce the Industry Secretary's salary and the discussion motion on the Public Expenditure White Paper, both Supply votes), and 1978; on adjournment motions following debates on specific topics in 1950, 1976, and 1977 (three times), and on various procedural motions in 1924, 1950, 1965, and 1977, the latter being on the guillotine motion for the Scotland and Wales Bill, in consequence of which the Bill, in its original form, was lost.

Under this heading, there thus falls not only a large number of defeats on minor issues or those which may not require action by the Government (such as some adjournment motions), but also defeats on issues which, although not central to Government policy, are nevertheless important, as, for example, the comparatively recent defeats on the 1972 immigration rules, the 1973 Maplin Development Bill,

[35] HC Deb., Vol. 398, col. 1452.

[36] There have been exceptions, the most obvious recent example being Chamberlain in 1940, but such exceptions have been motivated by political considerations rather than constitutional requirements.

[37] See P. Norton, 'Intra-Party Dissent in the House of Commons: A Case Study, The Immigration Rules 1972', *Parliamentary Affairs*, 29 (1976), 404–20.

[38] See HC Deb., XLIII, cols. 1773–8, 2053–4; HC Deb., XLIV, cols. 36–41 and 251–6; also Sir Edward Cadogan, *Before the Deluge* (1961), pp. 210–11.

the 1974 Finance Bill (three Opposition amendments to which cost, according to Government estimates, nearly £500 million[39]), the Government's Public Expenditure White Papers in 1976 and 1977, the 1976 Dock Work Regulation Bill, the guillotine motion for the Scotland and Wales Bill, the various amendments to the Scotland Bill (1977/8), a public inquiry into the Crown Agents' affair (1977), and the devaluation of the Green Pound (1978).

Given the nature of most divisions in the Commons, and the political consideration attached to such matters by the Government, Government defeats in the division lobbies will normally fall into this third category. Defeats involving questions of confidence in the Government are very much the exception, not the rule. It may be that if Government defeats falling within this third category nevertheless occur persistently, the Government may consider its ability to govern is impaired, but that is a matter for political—rather than constitutional—judgement. As long as the Government retains the confidence of the House, it may, at its discretion, remain in office until the statutory five-year maximum for the life of the Parliament is reached.

[39] HC Deb., Vol. 877, col. 395.

6

COLLECTIVE MINISTERIAL RESPONSIBILITY AND COLLECTIVE SOLIDARITY

DAVID L. ELLIS

INTRODUCTION

Inherent in any classical definition of the doctrine of collective ministerial responsibility are the twin facets of Government unanimity and accountability to Parliament.

Lord Salisbury in 1878 set out a formulation of the doctrine which has come to be accepted as the *locus classicus*:

> For all that passes in Cabinet every member of it who does not resign is absolutely and irretrievably responsible and has no right afterwards to say that he agreed in one case to a compromise, while in another he was persuaded by his colleagues. . . . It is only on the principle that absolute responsibility is undertaken by every member of the Cabinet, who, after a decision is arrived at, remains a member of it, that the joint responsibility of Ministers to Parliament can be upheld and one of the most essential principles of Parliamentary responsibility established.[1]

Professor Ivor Jennings, in his authoritative *Cabinet Government*, adopts Joseph Chamberlain's definition which emphasizes three points not explicitly stated in Lord Salisbury's formulation. First, the need for full and frank discussion in government; secondly, that not only should a minister resist seeking to disavow his own involvement in a past decision, but he must go further by giving his 'loyal support' thereto; thirdly, all decisions should be considered as being made by the Government as a whole.[2]

Abridged from *Public Law* (1980). Reprinted by permission of Stevens & Sons Limited.

[1] *Hansard*, 8 Apr. 1878, cols. 833–4.
[2] I. Jennings, *Cabinet Government* (3rd edn., 1965), p. 277. See also P. G. Walker,

THE UNANIMOUS FRONT OF THE GOVERNMENT

If Ministers remain in office after the taking of a decision and are to be held jointly responsible, then necessarily they must be seen to speak with one voice.

In 1940 Winston Churchill gave public support to Neville Chamberlain even though there were many who wished to see Churchill as Prime Minister. In 1950 a junior Minister criticized the Government's agricultural policy and then resigned. He was criticized by *The Economist* as follows: 'He would have been in a stronger position if he had resigned first and made his criticisms afterwards, rather than transgress an accepted rule of the constitution.'[3] In 1958 the public received no indication of a disagreement in Cabinet sufficiently serious to lead to the resignation of the Chancellor of the Exchequer.

An added element of flexibility in the rules of Government unanimity was introduced by the Wilson Government in 1967 in the form of the Green Paper. The intention was that whilst the Government might state its policy, differences of opinion might be expressed and changes made. White Papers were still to deal with major issues including manifesto commitments. Problems arose when Mrs Castle was seeking to introduce industrial relations policy and dissension was rife within the Cabinet. The relevant White Paper, *In Place of Strife*, was published as a basis for 'discussion', and hence bore similarities to a Green Paper. After public ministerial expressions of opposition, Mr Wilson began to have second thoughts as to whether collective responsibility should not also apply to Green Papers. Mr Wilson rebutted Mr Crossman's argument that those paragraphs in the White Paper which dealt with sanctions enforceable against strikers should be 'green edged' so as to enable discussion. He went as far as to state that the convention would be rigorously applied to all contents of all White Papers and even of Green Papers.[4]

As so often the case in the recent existence of collective responsibility, political expedience dictated a very different

The Cabinet (1970), p. 30, for a definition which stresses that a Government member must not only 'tacitly' accept a Cabinet decision, but must if necessary openly defend it.

[3] *The Economist*, 22 Apr. 1950.   [4] *The Guardian*, 5 Apr. 1969.

solution several years later. In the EEC Referendum debate of January 1975, Harold Wilson had no reservation in stating to the House of Commons that the White Paper outlining the proposals 'will have some "green edges" and I am prepared to discuss with the leader of the Opposition the basis on which advice will be given to the House on the Referendum'.[5] A new political stratagem by Harold Wilson to maintain Cabinet 'unity' and remain in power. meant a fresh interpretation of the malleable if not mythical convention.

A rationale for an expression of unanimity can be found in the words of Sir John Hunt, Cabinet Secretary: 'Ministers will not feel free frankly to discuss and to surrender their personal and departmental preference to the achievement of a common view, nor can they be expected to abide by a common decision, if they know that the stand they have taken and the points they have surrendered will sooner rather than later become public knowledge.'[6] In times of emergency, another reason for remaining united is that disagreement is the last thing a government can afford and hence a 'don't rock the boat' attitude develops. Dalton apparently considered resignation from the wartime coalition at the end of 1944, but took it for granted that such an expression of disagreement was not morally justified while the outcome of the war was still uncertain.[7] It might be argued that unanimity creates the impression that Ministers are working together which promotes greater electoral and party confidence, as well as enhancing the Government image in the eyes of foreign politicians, investors, and others.[8]

What evidence exists that there is a belief that ministers are under an obligation not to breach the rules of unanimity? In the House of Lords debate which followed the announcement of the 1932 'agreement to differ' Lord Peel declared: 'This

[5] HC Deb., col. 1750 (23 Jan. 1975).

[6] H. Young, *The Crossman Affair*, p. 14; the same view is expressed by Lord Gardiner in affidavit evidence for the Att.-Gen., ibid., pp. 70, 71.

[7] R. K. Alderman and J. A. Cross, *The Tactics of Resignation: A Study in British Cabinet Government* (1967), p. 16.

[8] J. Haines, Press Secretary to Harold Wilson from Jan. 1969 to Apr. 1976, states in *The Politics of Power* (1977), p. 158: 'The long climb back by Wilson from 1974 to 1976 was due to the creation not only of the public image of an experienced team of ministers, but also a real "team spirit" in government. This regained the credit that had been lost.'

matter of cabinet responsibility is not merely a convention[9] which can be discarded when required. It is in my judgment far more than a convention, because it is based upon common sense.'[10] Lord Widgery CJ in the decision in *Att.-Gen.* v. *Jonathan Cape*[11] stated: 'I find overwhelming evidence that the doctrine of joint responsibility is generally understood and practised, and equally strong evidence that it is on occasion ignored.' In cross-examination in the *Crossman Diaries* case Sir John Hunt in reply to the question whether he regarded collective responsibility as a convention[12] stated 'no', because he thought it should be regarded as a 'reality and an important part of the constitution'.

COLLECTIVE DECISION-MAKING — REALITY AND MYTH

In theory at least it is not necessary for the preservation of collective responsibility that each Minister, particularly those who are senior and members of the Cabinet, should be given the opportunity to discuss governmental policy. The critical fact is that once the decision has been made there should be no sign of dissension. The reality of collective decision-taking is that it is still regarded as the accepted practice of Cabinet government. However, the emergence of Prime Ministerial government,[13] government by Inner Cabinet,[14] and so forth has done much to alter this impression. The significance of these changes in the style of government can be illustrated by

[9] I submit that this is a mistaken use of the term 'convention' as previously defined in this paper. Substitution of the word 'usage' would be more correct.

[10] HL Deb., col. 538 (10 Feb. 1932). [11] [1976] 1 QB 752, 770B.

[12] Problems arose in the case over the definition of convention supplied by Professor Wade, namely, an obligation founded in *conscience* only. Witnesses for the Att.-Gen.'s case were constantly striving to establish a level of obligation higher than mere conscience, but inferior to legal sanction.

[13] e.g. R. Crossman, *Inside View* (1970)—control of Cabinet proceedings by postponement of decision-taking; cf. Haines, op. cit., p. 9, and H. Wilson, *Governance of Britain* (1976), p. 52, R. Crossman, *Diaries of a Cabinet Minister*, i (1975), 350, criticism of Seamen's Union—disregarded by PM in public speech of Cabinet attitude.

[14] e.g. Crossman *Diaries*, i. 290—'What happened there was as near to central dictatorship as one is likely to get in a British Cabinet'; ibid. 515—'But on Rhodesia, when the Cabinet gets going, the P.M. just sits and chats. We occasionally ask him a question and the meeting disintegrates into amiable discussion, because all the decisions are taken by the P.M. and his little group behind the scenes.' (12 May 1966)—Sanctions Busting?

the following extract from the *Richard Crossman Diaries* dated December 1968:

This computer thing is yet another example of the complete departmentalism of our cabinet. Harold Wilson has got it all nicely in a corner with Tony Wedgwood Benn, Denis Healey and Tony Crosland, just as I have my whole corner without interference. Well there are worse ways of running a government, but it does destroy the effectiveness of collective cabinet responsibility. It looks as though he has had enough of that for some time.[15]

There are many other factors which can cause a Minister to feel frustrated over his lack of true 'responsibility' for the decisions taken. It may be judged expedient by certain Ministers to take the decision themselves without reporting the matter to Cabinet.[16] In late June 1973 the National Executive Committee of the Labour party unanimously passed a resolution protesting against a test explosion which was not apparently decided in full Cabinet. Some Ministers, infuriated at being left out of the decision-making process, joined in this vote, condemning a government action for which they shared responsibility since they had all stayed in office. Certain Government offices are fairly independent of criticism, especially on certain issues. The Foreign Office can often function without considerable outside restraint because Ministers simply do not have the time to keep abreast of external affairs which would require the reading of a substantial amount of FO telegrams. The departmentalization within Cabinet means that Ministers are also often uninformed on problems in other quarters[17] and even lack the energy to participate fully in Cabinet.[18] Furthermore, in the

[15] Crossman, *Diaries*, iii. 295 (23 Dec. 1969).

[16] Crossman, *Diaries*, i. 414: He was considering planning permission for Canvey Island development. Whilst normally he would have decided the matter personally, he was persuaded by Dame Evelyn (Permanent Secretary) that the matter was sufficiently important to put before Cabinet. He regretted that he was 'duly overridden by the collective decision.'

[17] e.g. R. Marsh, *Off the Rails* (1978), chap. 6, 'Life in the Cabinet', p. 88, refers to the sheer breadth of work and that no minister was able to give a full progress report; ibid. 89–90. Haines, op. cit., p. 12, 'cocooned within their departments, it is astonishing how politically maladroit some ministers can be'.

[18] B. Headley, *British Cabinet Ministers* (1974), p. 38, Table 2.2, 'Problems in the Organisation of Ministerial Time': The largest percentage of ministers questioned stated that the activity requiring more time was 'deciding major policy issues'; second most important task was attendance at Cabinet and Cabinet Committees.

Labour Governments of the 1960s and 1970s with which I am particularly concerned, Cabinet Ministers were obligated to follow the dictates of the mandate from the Labour Party Conference. Richard Crossman has written: 'In our cabinet discussion when a minister can claim his proposal is in the mandate, the others dare not say "no." '[19] The secrecy which surrounds Budget proposals and the catastrophic consequences of the resignation by a Chancellor of the Exchequer means that Ministers' criticisms are restricted in areas of economic management.[20]

What then is the practical effect on the unity of Cabinet where there is this build-up of frustration at the lack of ministerial influence on decision-taking? The facts surrounding the episode which led to the resignation of George Brown in March 1968 are still confused. The essential point however is clear enough, namely that the decision to devalue the pound was taken at a meeting of the Privy Council at which Brown, the then Foreign Secretary, was absent. The explanation for his resignation related by Brown to the *Sunday Times* read as follows: '. . . it has been actuated by a conviction lying deep in the gut that Wilson's method of politics and government are especially intolerable . . . there is the disruptive technique of government by clique and standards of decision making have deteriorated.'[21] Another indication that an authoritarian style of government thwarts unity and collective responsibility is provided by the criticism directed at the Australian Prime Minister, Malcolm Fraser. His method of government caused irritation to the point where the stability of his leadership was in question. The major criticisms were his tendency to make all the decisions and display little loyalty towards colleagues 'in trouble'.[22]

[19] Crossman, *Inside View*, p. 98.

[20] Crossman, *Diaries*, i. 511: 'By far the most important aspect of this budget is the constitutional issue. It seems to me to make an absolute mockery of Cabinet government and Cabinet responsibility to introduce S.E.T. in this way and tell none of us about it until it is too late to do anything.'

[21] *Sunday Times*, 17 Mar. 1968; cf. Crossman, *Diaries*, ii. 714, commenting on the Brown resignation as follows: 'If I was ever to resign it would be precisely because I can't stand the way Cabinet is run.' Wilson, 'The Labour Government 1964–70', retaliated that Brown's stance had only a few days prior to his resignation been such as to suggest to Wilson that the latter should refer *fewer* major issues for collective decisions.   [22] *The Times*, 7 Nov. 1978.

The question that must now be answered is: to what extent changes in decision-making have eroded Cabinet power, and the consequent effect upon collective responsibility. Writing in 1974 David Butler, having considered the operation of the doctrine in England and Australia, concluded that 'cabinet in both countries seems to have a remarkable vitality'.[23] Mr Gordon Walker argued in his text that Harold Wilson was far from always getting his own way.[24] Richard Marsh was also quick to criticize Crossman's formulation of Prime Ministerial government as simply not being borne out by the facts of episodes such as the failure of the 1969 Industrial Relations Bill.[25] I would submit that though numerous exceptions to the practice of collective decision-making can be cited, there are very few illustrations which show a critical exclusion of Ministers by procedural manipulation. None of these incidents is sufficiently serious that one might consider collective responsibility as being threatened by a Minister so irate at being excluded from cabinet that he might bring the disagreement into the public eye. The importance for collective responsibility of ensuring Cabinet compliance is illustrated in a significant review by Harold Wilson of Crossman's 'Godkin Lectures': 'The Prime Minister's task is to get a consensus of Cabinet or he cannot reasonably ask for loyalty and collective responsibility.'[26] Another practical example of the doctrine affecting the rules of Cabinet decision-making is that under collective responsibility every vote counts equal, on the reasoning that each Minister assumes the same responsibility. This application of the convention has been generally criticized[27] as outdated in that Cabinet decisions are often highly technical and insufficient weight is given by this method of voting to those members conversant with the issue. This example reflects collective responsibility assuming the character of a binding convention, able to survive into the twentieth century despite its anachronistic application.

[23] D. Butler, *Ministerial Responsibility in England and Australia* (1974), p. 410.
[24] G. Walker, *The Cabinet* (2nd edn., 1972).
[25] Marsh, op. cit.
[26] *New Statesman*, 5 May 1972.
[27] Marsh, op. cit., p. 91.

GOVERNMENT OFFICE AND THE RULES OF COLLECTIVE RESPONSIBILITY

If collective responsibility is to be a reality, then a Minister will not be able to express public disagreement with Government policy and remain in office. The general rule, however, in the 1960s and 1970s is that Cabinet Ministers do not always leave office merely because they have openly disagreed with Cabinet policy. In the past there was generally no public disagreement and if an individual Minister could not bring himself to lend open support to a Cabinet decision, he had no option but to resign and then disclose his reasons. Thus Anthony Eden resigned in 1938 because he disagreed with the policy of appeasement. Aneurin Bevan resigned in 1951[28] over NHS charges and a year later he was breaching the rules of collective responsibility *ex post facto*, by revealing that he was personally responsible for an aspect of the Government's rearmament programme in 1950. The day after this revelation, Atlee confronted Bevan with the convention of Cabinet secrecy. There is a convention that upon resignation a Minister may obtain the Sovereign's permission to disclose the reasons for leaving office. This inevitably detracts from collective responsibility. Bevan compounded this incursion on collective responsibility, first because he neither sought nor obtained permission to make any disclosure and secondly, because the adoption of the defence programme was not the point over which he had resigned. Here again, as with so many aspects of the convention, it can be breached with impunity if the only possible sanction is a poor conscience.

Today malcontent Ministers play a much more devious game than their predecessors and inevitably subject collective responsibility to greater pressure.[29] Often the public disagreement is superficially resolved by a public apology;[30] alternatively Ministers may leak Cabinet material and remain

---

[28] For a full list of ministerial resignations on policy grounds (1900–67), see Alderman and Cross, op. cit., The Appendix.

[29] Dec. 1976, Prentice was an exception—politically alienated in Cabinet, he was forced to resign over policy differences.

[30] As in the case of Callaghan and the NEC.

anonymous. If they do decide to oppose the Prime Minister openly, Cabinet Ministers will probably have the power and influence to do so and remain in office.[31] Admittedly, during the Benn–Callaghan clash in October 1978,[32] the former stated that he would resign if Britain entered the EMS. Resign he did not, but had he done so, it would have been because he could not stomach Cabinet policy and felt frustrated at being unable to influence events, rather than because he felt that resignation was dictated by the convention. He did not seem troubled by his open disagreement with his Cabinet colleagues, nor by the possibility that collective responsibility would mean that he was partly responsible for the decision to enter the EMS.

Yet another ministerial stance which threatens collective responsibility is to disagree, but then not push for any sort of show-down. In 1928 Lord Birkenhead while introducing his Government's measure to reduce the voting age of women declared that he was opposed to female suffrage. However, had he resigned every time that his 'wise and advantageous advice' was rejected, he argued he would seldom have been in office.[33] From 1964 to 1966, Frank Cousins was a Cabinet Minister in a government which was formulating an incomes policy opposed by the Trade Union of which he was the General Secretary *in absentia*. It was suggested that his studied disinclination to commend publicly his colleagues' proposals was a breach of collective responsibility. Bernard Crick[34] responded with a proposition that is probably nearer the truth of Cabinet practice today—'the doctrine while involving the avoidance of public disagreement, had never meant the suppression of implied reservations'. Irrespective of whether or not it was a breach of the convention, Mr Cousins ended the dilemma a year later by resigning.

The application of collective responsibility is more rigid towards junior Government members than it is to senior Cabinet Ministers. The application of the doctrine to non-Cabinet Ministers is very much a twentieth-century develop-

---

[31] Marsh, op. cit., p. 93—'There were many rows but it is very difficult for a P.M. to discipline one of his colleagues in public.'

[32] *The Times*, 24 Oct. 1978.

[33] HL Deb., Vol. 71, cols. 252, 253.   [34] *The Observer*, 28 July 1965.

ment. Gladstone was prepared to allow greater freedom to Government members not actually involved in the making of decisions by the Cabinet. More recent examples in this particular area include the resignation of Eric Heffer in 1975.[35] On 20 November 1978 Mr Robert Cryer resigned as Under-Secretary of State at the Department of Industry in protest at the decision to cut off public funds to the Kirkby Workers' Co-operative.

In 1969 Dr. Jeremy Bray[36] sought to publish a book on the machinery of Government. Harold Wilson requested Bray's resignation, not because of any policy disagreement, but to uphold the principles of collective responsibility. The rationale offered was the need to prevent Ministers from running off in different directions and to ensure opinions were pressed only within the Government machine.[37] I suggest that there is no justification in such a rigid adherence to this level of technicality at a time when collective responsibility is threatened in far more important areas.

Should collective responsibility be applied to the relatively lowly levels of Parliamentary State Secretaries (PPSs), who are not even Ministers, but unpaid aides to individual Ministers?[38] Most of the arguments for and against recently surfaced after the dismissal of Brian Sedgemore. He held the post of PPS to Mr Benn and was sacked for disclosing the contents of a confidential Treasury brief at a Commons Select Committee meeting.[39] As might be expected the NEC took an interest in this matter, after all, the effect of imposing dismissal on PPSs is to extend collective responsibility within Government from about 100 to 140 people. Neil Kinnock MP, newly elected executive member, suggested that the Parliamentary Labour Party should in due course consider whether an essentially personal loyalty of service from a PPS to a Minister should enter the penumbra of collective responsibility. The suggested test should be that if a PPS came upon

[35] For further examples see S. A. de Smith, *Constitutional and Administrative Law* (3rd edn., 1977), p. 171.
[36] Joint Parliamentary Secretary at the Ministry of Technology.
[37] *The Times*, 26 Sept. 1969; reply by Bray in *The Times*, 29 Sept. 1969, p. 11.
[38] For examples, see de Smith, op. cit., p. 171.
[39] *The Times*, 23 Nov. 1978, suggests that there is no justification in principle for collective responsibility to apply to PPSs.

information as an MP rather than in his capacity as PPS, he should be free to use it. There is much to commend this proposition, especially at a time when collective responsibility, having been defeated in certain spheres, is seeking to thrust itself, almost without justification, into other developing areas of the Constitution.

In general, PPSs are particularly susceptible to dismissal, since they lack influence and power to defend themselves. However, if a sufficient number act in concert, they can rely on strength of numbers to reduce the potency of collective responsibility. In December 1974 eight PPSs were among fifty-four rebellious Labour MPs. Mr Wilson's refusal to discipline the PPSs almost led to Mr Mellish resigning as Government Chief Whip. The rule once again appears to be that if you are powerful enough or if there are no effective sanctions imposable against you, the convention of collective responsibility is an easy hurdle to surmount, if it exists at all.

7

THE 'AGREEMENT TO DIFFER' OF 1975

ARTHUR SILKIN

Although the doctrine of ministerial responsibility is not to be found in any Act of Parliament, it has for almost 200 years been one of the corner-stones of British constitutional practice. The term itself is, of course, used in two different, if related, senses. *Collective* ministerial responsibility means that any decisions taken by the Cabinet are binding on all Ministers, whether members of the Cabinet or not, and any Minister who disagrees with them is expected either to remain silent or to resign. The essential meaning of *individual* ministerial responsibility is that the Minister is the political spokesman of his department and is answerable before Parliament for its policies and administration. These two doctrines have as their corollaries, first, that the departmental Minister cannot have a policy which diverges from that of the Cabinet to which he belongs or owes allegiance and, secondly, that, in so far as he is required to speak publicly as his department's representative on this policy, whether in Parliament or outside it, he must support it. The obverse of these doctrines is that, once a final decision on policy has been made, the actions and policy statements of departmental civil servants must conform with the views both of the political head of the department and of the Government as a whole.

EARLY BREACHES OF CONVENTION

Breaches of the convention have occurred over the years but, with the exception of the 'agreement to differ' of January 1932, about which more will be said shortly, these have been both

From *The Political Quarterly*, 46 (1977), 65–73. © The Political Quarterly Publishing Co. Ltd. Reprinted by permission of Basil Blackwell Limited.

unofficial and of relatively minor significance. Although there
have doubtless been other instances, two are of particular
interest in that they consist of open or implied criticisms
of agreed Government policies by senior Ministers not
themselves responsible for the departmental policies on which
they pronounced and without clearing their speeches with
either the Cabinet or the departmental Ministers concerned.
The first was on 10 June 1936, when Mr Neville Chamberlain,
at that time Chancellor of the Exchequer, described the
continuance or intensification of sanctions against Italy as the
'very midsummer of madness'. Mr Baldwin, the Prime
Minister, when questioned about this speech, said that no
decision on the future of sanctions had been reached.[1] A
somewhat similar instance of a Minister speaking out of turn
occurred when Mr James Callaghan was Home Secretary and
had, therefore, no departmental responsibility for the Government's wages policy. This did not, however, prevent him from
publicly stating his view in May 1968 that by the autumn of
1969 the then existing statutory wages policy would be
replaced by a voluntary one; Mr Wilson, the then Prime
Minister, specifically dissociated himself and the Cabinet
from Mr Callaghan's view.[2] It seems likely that both Mr
Chamberlain and Mr Callaghan were deliberately seeking to
pre-empt a major change in government policy, though how
far the changes in policy which subsequently took place were
due to these 'pre-emptive strikes' and how far they would have
taken place in any case can only be conjectured. More
recently, in March 1974, a number of Ministers, including one
Cabinet Minister, Mr Benn, publicly criticized the decision of
the recently elected Labour Government to permit the sale of
four frigates to Chile.[3]

THE 'AGREEMENT TO DIFFER' OF 1932

These infringements of the convention of collective ministerial
responsibility, consisting as they did of spontaneous actions

---

[1] *Manchester Guardian*, 12 June 1936.   [2] *The Times*, 30 May 1968.
[3] *The Times*, 2 and 9 May 1974. The other Ministers concerned were Mr Eric
Heffer, who led the attack, Mrs Judith Hart, a senior departmental Minister though
not a member of the Cabinet, and Miss Joan Lestor, who was at the time a Minister
at the Foreign and Commonwealth Office, the department which was primarily
responsible for the very policy which Miss Lestor was criticizing.

by individual Ministers and not of an agreed arrangement by the Government as a whole, have nothing in common with the Cabinet decision of April 1975 officially to allow Ministers who disagreed with the Government over the Common Market a limited right to express views at variance with those of the Government. The only precedent for this arrangement is that of the so-called 'agreement to differ' of 22 January 1932, which arose out of disagreements between Ministers of the National Government over the levy of tariff duties. During the General Election campaign of October 1931 candidates who supported the National Government had agreed not to oppose one another[4] in spite of the fact that the tariff duties which the Conservative party advocated as a solution of the economic difficulties were bitterly opposed by most members of other parties, and particularly by the Liberals. In order to avoid a split it was agreed that each candidate should be free to advocate his own remedies. There was never any likelihood that the disagreement between the parties over what was regarded at the time as an issue of fundamental importance would vanish after the election, and it did not do so. Indeed, following a report of a Cabinet Committee proposing a general tariff, four members of the Cabinet handed in their resignations; they were, however, persuaded to withdraw them when the Cabinet accepted the proposal of Mr Ramsay MacDonald, the Prime Minister, that they should as an exceptional measure be allowed to express their dissent publicly by speech and vote in view of the paramount importance of maintaining national unity. (*The Times*, 23 January 1932, gives the full text of the official statement embodying the Cabinet decision.)

This decision was described by Mr Harold Macmillan as a 'curious device, unprecedented in politics';[5] as he pointed out, the rather similar formula, 'used in many Cabinets in the first quarter of the nineteenth century to deal with the vexed question of Catholic emancipation, was merely an agreement to hold different views upon a question on which legislation was not proposed'.

Although Sir Herbert Samuel, the Home Secretary and one

[1] Sir Ivor Jennings, *Cabinet Government* (3rd edn., 1965), pp. 279 ff.
[5] H. Macmillan, *Winds of Change, 1914–1939*.

of the four dissentient Ministers,[6] was taken to task by Conservative supporters of the National Government for allegedly widening the area of disagreement in a House of Commons debate on the trade balance on 4 February,[7] this was very much an isolated incident and, with that single exception, the dissident Ministers, Sir Herbert Samuel included, refrained from making any general criticism of the National Government's policy until they all resigned over the decision to give effect to the Ottawa agreements on imperial preference on 28 September 1932.

THE REFERENDUM CAMPAIGN: RIGHT TO DISSENT

Mr Harold Wilson's announcement giving Ministers who disagreed with the Government's recommendation that the United Kingdom should remain in the Common Market a limited freedom to advocate their views during the referendum campaign was made on 7 April 1975, when he said, in reply to a written question:

In accordance with my statement in the House on January 23 last, those Ministers who do not agree with the Government's recommendation in favour of continued membership of the European Community are, in the unique circumstances of the referendum, now free to advocate a different view during the referendum campaign in the country.

This freedom does not extend to parliamentary proceedings and official business. Government business in Parliament will continue to be handled by all Ministers in accordance with Government policy. Ministers responsible for European aspects of Government business who themselves differ from the Government's recommendation on membership of the European Community will state the Government's position and will not be drawn into making points against the Government recommendations. Whenever necessary, Questions will be transferred to other Ministers. At meetings of the Council of Ministers of the European Community and at other

---

[6] The others were Lord Snowden, Lord Privy Seal, Sir Donald Maclean, President of the Board of Education, and Sir Archibald Sinclair, Secretary of State for Scotland. All of these were Liberals except for Lord Snowden, who was a former Labour Chancellor of the Exchequer.

[7] *The Times*, 5 and 9 Feb. 1932. Referring to the same incident, Mr Harold Macmillan, op. cit., described Sir Herbert Samuel as 'making a violent and extremely forceful attack upon the folly of his colleagues'.

Community meetings the United Kingdom position in all fields will continue to reflect Government policy.

I have asked all Ministers to make their contributions to the public campaign in terms of issues, to avoid personalising or trivialising the argument, and not to allow themselves to appear in direct confrontation, on the same platform or programme, with another Minister who takes a different view on the Government recommendation.

DIFFERENCES BETWEEN 1932 AND 1975

Superficially alike as the two 'agreements to differ' were, there were important differences between them. In 1932 dissident Ministers were allowed to make their disagreement known from the Treasury Bench itself. In 1975 this procedure was not officially permitted, the Prime Minister's explanation for this being that in 1932 the only opportunity for dissident Ministers to make their views known was through a debate in the House whereas the decision to hold a referendum in 1975 enabled Ministers who opposed the Government decision to campaign publicly in favour of withdrawal from the EEC. In practice, as we shall see shortly, this restriction was easily circumvented by the dissentients. Secondly, none of the dissident Ministers in 1932 had any departmental responsibility for issues connected with the official area of disagreement;[8] this was palpably not true of 1975. Thirdly, the area of the 1975 disagreement was in practice broadened, at any rate while the referendum campaign was in progress, to cover issues extraneous to the EEC, whereas the differences arising out of the 1932 agreement appear, with the one possible exception already mentioned, to have been limited to the area for which these special arrangements had been made, that of protective tariffs. There was, however, a fourth difference, possibly of greater potential significance than the others. Whereas the 1932 arrangements covered Ministers of different parties, who were, at least in original intention, united for a limited purpose and duration, those of 1975

---

[8] As already indicated, the offices of the dissentient Ministers were Lord Privy Seal, Home Secretary, President of the Board of Education, and Secretary of State for Scotland.

concerned members of the same political party. It therefore sanctified the idea that Ministers of the same political party could publicly disagree over important issues, even though admittedly for a limited duration, while still remaining Ministers.

EFFECTS ON COLLECTIVE MINISTERIAL RESPONSIBILITY

It was not long before the first crack in the 'agreement to differ' appeared. On 9 April, only two days after the Prime Minister's announcement, thirty-eight Ministers, including Whips, among them seven Cabinet Ministers, voted against a House of Commons motion to approve the EEC renegotiation White Paper. As this was on a free vote, the action of the dissident Ministers did not in itself offend against either the letter or the spirit of the Prime Minister's announcement. Mr Eric Heffer's case was altogether different. He had already a year earlier been the prime mover in the campaign against the Government's decision to sell frigates to Chile. Now he openly defied the Government's guidelines for the conduct of Ministers during the referendum campaign by going to the back-benches to attack Government policy, thereby courting and securing instant dismissal from his post. Meanwhile, one of the most senior Cabinet Ministers, Mr Benn, Secretary of State for Industry, appears to have made use of the 'agreement to differ' on a number of occasions in order to publicize his political and personal disagreements with his Cabinet colleagues. The first such occasion was on 22 April, within 24 hours of the end of the Budget debate, in which the Chancellor of the Exchequer, Mr Healey, had been urging the need for demand to be reduced. According to an article by Nora Beloff in *The Observer*, 27 April 1975, Mr Benn thereupon circulated a paper to the seventy members of the Labour party's Industrial Sub-Committee, in which he recommended the diametrically opposite policy of reflation, only to have these views subsequently repudiated by the Prime Minister himself. It is indeed possible to argue that this extension of the area of disagreement had nothing to do with the 'agreement to differ' as it had been widely reported that Mr Benn and the

Prime Minister had already had a major disagreement the previous summer over Mr Benn's White Paper on the regeneration of British industry. However that may be, Mr Benn's disagreement with the Chancellor's policy in April 1975 appears to have been both more open and more deliberate than his earlier disagreement with Mr Wilson over his White Paper. The second occasion was when, on 7 May, he clashed with Mrs Shirley Williams, Secretary of State for Prices and Consumer Protection, at a meeting of the National Economic Development Council (NEDC). It seems that, after Mrs Williams had attributed much of the responsibility for the country's current investment difficulties to the tendency of successive Administrations to reverse the policies of their predecessors, Mr Benn went out of his way to dissociate himself from his Cabinet colleague's views.[9] The third occasion was in a speech on the Industry Bill in the House of Commons on 14 May, when Mr Benn, admittedly in the heat of the moment, criticized fellow-members of his own Government for their alleged unconcern about the danger of unemployment, although he almost immediately retracted the accusation. Another example of bickering between members of the Government should be mentioned as, even though this took place in the context of discussions about the EEC and did not, therefore, involve a widening of the area of conflict, it did occur in a debate in the House of Commons and was, therefore, a contravention of the strict terms of the agreement of 7 April. This was Mr Roy Jenkins's statement on 27 May that he found it 'increasingly difficult to take Mr Benn seriously as an Economics Minister'.[10] The terms of Mr Jenkins's criticism of Mr Benn are of interest not so much for themselves as because they seemed to be an echo of an earlier criticism of one Cabinet Minister by another. This was the accusation of 'economic illiteracy' levelled against the Secretary of State for Education and Science, Mr Prentice, on 1 March 1975, well before the 'agreement to differ' had been

---

[9] *The Times*, 8 May 1975.

[10] *The Times*, 28 May 1975. Mr Healey had also attacked Mr Benn on the same grounds two days earlier, though without referring to him by name—see *The Times*, 26 May 1975.

announced, by Mr Michael Foot, his Cabinet colleague at the Department of Employment.[11]

It has already been shown that the limited agreement to differ over the Common Market issue was, perhaps inevitably, very quickly broadened into public disagreements by Cabinet Ministers over a considerably wider area. In addition, it soon became apparent that the restrictions which Mr Wilson had imposed on Ministers 'not to allow themselves to appear in direct confrontation, on the same platform or programme, with another Minister who takes a different view on the Government recommendation' were unworkable. Indeed, Mr Wilson himself explicitly recognized this when on 23 May he relaxed his original ministerial guidelines so as to enable Ministers to put the case for and against the EEC on the same programme provided the interviews were pre-recorded and there was no direct confrontation in the same studio. So far as the last four days of the referendum campaign were concerned, however, a further relaxation was introduced under which Ministers were allowed to take part in 'live' programmes to argue the differing points of view. It was under these arrangements that the leading protagonists of the two points of view in the Cabinet, Mr Jenkins and Mr Benn, staged a direct confrontation in the BBC programme 'Panorama' three days before the date of the referendum.

EFFECTS ON INDIVIDUAL RESPONSIBILITY

The terms of the Prime Minister's guidelines suggested that he foresaw that the 'agreement to differ' would be likely to lead to some breaches in the doctrine that Ministers were the spokesmen of their departments' policy, both inside and outside Parliament. It was for this reason that his written answer on 7 April, while emphasizing that the freedom afforded to Ministers to advocate a view different from that of the Government during the referendum campaign in the country did not extend to parliamentary proceedings and official business, nevertheless made provision for questions addressed to dissentient Ministers to be transferred, where

[11] *The Economist*, 8 Mar. 1975.

necessary, to other Ministers. This was all the more necessary because two of the dissentients, Mr Benn, Secretary of State for Industry, and Mr Shore, Secretary of State for Trade, were in posts which it required no great foresight to predict would be likely to involve them in answering Opposition questions about the EEC which were specifically designed to draw attention to their differences with the Government, while a third, Mr Michael Foot, Secretary of State for Employment, might also be expected, if to a lesser degree, to be subjected to hostile questioning on the same issue. The other dissident Cabinet Ministers—Mrs Castle, Secretary of State for Social Services, Mr Ross, Secretary of State for Scotland, Mr John Silkin, Minister for Local Government and Planning, and Mr Varley, Secretary of State for Energy—were, because of the nature of their work, much less likely to be required to answer embarrassing questions.

In the event, the Prime Minister seriously underestimated the implications of this compromise. It was implicit in the terms of the guidelines that embarrassing questions addressed to dissident Ministers would either be transferred to another Minister or that the reply to the questions themselves would be drafted or at any rate approved by the Foreign and Commonwealth Office. In actual fact, during the seven weeks between the Prime Minister's announcement and Parliament going into extended recess to allow Ministers and MPs to take part in the referendum campaign, seven questions on EEC matters were transferred from the department to which they were originally addressed. There is nothing in the least unusual in the transfer of questions from one department to another and the fact that these seven questions were so transferred is in itself scarcely a matter for comment. Potentially much more serious were the constitutional considerations implicit in those instances in which anti-EEC Ministers themselves replied to questions on the EEC. While the replies to the original questions had to be cleared with the Foreign and Commonwealth Office and were not, therefore, at variance with Government policy, the same was not, of course, true of the supplementary questions to which Ministers have to reply impromptu and which could not in the nature of things be cleared in advance with the Foreign and

Commonwealth Office, even supposing—a very doubtful supposition—that anti-EEC Ministers would have been prepared to sacrifice the opportunity of a supplementary question to express their own personal views on the EEC issue in the larger interests of strict adherence to the Government guidelines. This inevitably meant that the replies given by anti-EEC Ministers to some supplementary questions did not wholly conform with Government policy, while the answers they gave to others were clearly opposed to it. At Question Time on 21 April Mr Benn resorted to subterfuges in order to avoid open contradiction of official Government policy. For example, when asked by a Conservative Member whether the supplementary answer he had given to another MP had been approved by the Foreign Office, he said: 'I have nothing to add to the speech made by my right hon. friend the Member for Bristol, South-East, in other parts of the country.'[12] In giving this answer, he was in effect stating in the House of Commons that he continued to hold the anti-EEC views he had expressed—and been permitted by the guidelines to express—outside the House. Mr Shore, Secretary of State for Trade, was equally devious when it was his turn to answer oral questions on 5 May, so that it was not at first sight clear whether these Ministers were expressing personal views or those of the Government when responding to supplementary questions. Indeed, when he was specifically asked by a Conservative Member to say what he meant by 'we', Mr Shore gave the evasive answer: 'When I am speaking from the Dispatch Box I am reflecting Government policy as a whole, except when I am clearly reflecting my own policy as Secretary of State for Trade.' In other words, Mr Shore at no stage admitted that he was voicing his own opinions as an anti-Marketeer, which would, of course, have been outside the terms of the Government guidelines.

It was not, however, only in reply to supplementary questions during Question Time that anti-EEC Ministers found a way of making known their disagreement with Government policy over the EEC in the House of Commons. On 10 April Mr Heseltine, Opposition spokesman on industry,

[12] *Hansard*, 21 Apr. 1975. Mr Benn was, of course, himself the Right Hon. Member for Bristol, South-East.

wrote to Mr Wilson complaining that members of the Industry Bill Standing Commiteee were being placed in an impossible position by reason of the fact that all the Ministers on that committee were opposed to the Government view about membership of the EEC. This made a nonsense of the committee stage of the Bill, where 'clause after clause . . . have a relevance to the European relationship and its impact on industry'. Mr Benn also came in for some criticism when, on 6 May 1975, in a reply to a supplementary question to a Private Notice Question by Mr Heseltine on the steel industry, he pointedly declared that, under the Treaty of Paris, the United Kingdom steel industry would be controlled 'elsewhere'.

8

MINISTERS' MEMOIRS

THE RADCLIFFE COMMITTEE REPORT

SUMMARY OF CONCLUSIONS AND RECOMMENDATIONS

1. The conventions currently governing the publication by former Ministers of memoirs and other works relating to their experience as Ministers were laid down in a statement made in the House of Commons on 1 August 1946 on behalf of the Prime Minister (Mr Attlee) by the Lord President of the Council (Mr Herbert Morrison). This was based on a memorandum by the Secretary of the Cabinet, Sir Edward Bridges, which Mr Attlee's Cabinet had approved. (*Paragraphs 13, 14, 41, 42.*)

2. The conventions established in 1946 have been maintained under successive Administrations and the Committee do not recommend modification of the principles then advocated. They do however draw out of the conventions certain specific working rules: and make recommendations as to the administrative structure which should condition the clearance of the ex-Minister's intended memoirs. The conventions are to be regarded as concessions made to the author, rather than as restrictions imposed on him. (*Paragraphs 19, 38, 43.*)

3. The author should be free to use his ministerial experience for the purpose of giving an account of his own work, subject to restrictions on three separate categories of information:

1. He must not reveal anything that contravenes the requirements of national security operative at the time of his proposed publication.

2. He must not make disclosures injurious to this country's relations with other nations.

3. He must refrain from publishing information destructive

From Appendix 2, *Report of the Committee of Privy Councillors*, Cmnd. 6386 (1976). Reprinted by permission of Her Majesty's Stationery Office.

of the confidential relationships on which our system of government is based. In particular—

(a) In dealing with the experience that he has acquired by virtue of his official position, he should not reveal the opinions or attitudes of colleagues as to the Government business with which they have been concerned. That belongs to their stewardship, not to his. He may, on the other hand, describe and account for his own.

(b) He should not reveal the advice given to him by individuals whose duty it has been to tender him their advice or opinions in confidence. If he wishes to mention the burden or weight of such advice, it must be done without attributing individual attitudes to identifiable persons. Again, he will need to exercise a continuing discretion in any references that he makes to communications received by him in confidence from outside members of the public.

(c) He should not make public assessments or criticisms, favourable or unfavourable, of those who have served under him or those whose competence or suitability for particular posts he has had to measure as part of his official duties.

He may, however, regard the obligations concerned with confidential relationships (but not those concerned with national security and international relations) as lifted after the expiry of 15 years from the relevant events, though even beyond that point he should not reveal the advice tendered by individuals who are still members of the public services nor make public assessments or criticisms of them. (*Paragraphs 45–47, 83, 85, 86.*)

4. These restrictions leave him a wide latitude for the writing of an account of his stewardship. (*Paragraph 87.*)

5. The established principles of law do not provide a system which can protect and enforce those rules of reticence that the Committee regard as called for when ex-Ministers compose their memoirs of ministerial life. (*Paragraph 65.*)

6. Nor does legislation offer the right solution. (*Paragraph 69.*)

7. There can be no guarantee that, if the burden of

compliance is left to rest on the free acceptance of an obligation of honour, there will never be an occasional rebel or an occasional breach; but so long as there remains a general recognition of the practical necessity of some rules and the importance of observing them, the Committee do not think that such transgressions, even though made the subject of sensational publicity, should be taken as having shattered the fabric of a sensible system. (*Paragraph 69.*)

8. A Minister on taking and leaving office should have his attention drawn explicitly to his obligations in relation to memoirs. (*Paragraphs 71, 72.*)

9. A former Minister proposing to publish a work relating to his ministerial experience should submit the manuscript to the Secretary of the Cabinet. (*Paragraphs 73–7.*)

10. The Secretary of the Cabinet, acting at the request of the prime Minister and on his behalf, should have duties of two kinds in relation to such a manuscript. (*Paragraphs 77, 78.*)

1. *To have it examined in respect of national security and the preservation of international relations and to transmit any objections to the author.* The author should have a right of reference to the Prime Minister but should accept the latter's decision as final. (*Paragraph 79.*)

2. *To offer views on the treatment of confidential relationships in the manuscript.* The author should pay careful attention to this advice but must take upon his own shoulders the responsibility for deciding what he is going to say. If he decides to publish material in spite of advice from the Secretary of the Cabinet, he should let the Secretary know what he proposes to do so that before publication there may be time for the Prime Minister to bring his own direct influence to bear upon the dispute, if he wishes to do so. (*Paragraph 80.*)

11. A former Minister who has kept a diary of his ministerial experience should give testamentary instructions to ensure that its publication does not flout the current understandings that his own ex-colleagues are likely to be observing. (*Paragraph 99.*)

12. Former members of the public services should be under the same obligation as former Ministers to submit their manuscripts for scrutiny with regard to national security and international relations, and to defer to the judgement of those

carrying the immediate responsibilities in these fields. In the matter of confidential relationships, the principles which the Committee enunciate concerning publications by ex-Ministers, the obligations which they suggest should rest upon them, and the periods for which these obligations should be maintained, should all be reflected also in the rules governing the publication of memoirs and other works relating to their official experience by former members of the public services. (*Paragraphs 92, 93.*)

9

ACCESS TO A PREVIOUS GOVERNMENT'S PAPERS

LORD HUNT OF TANWORTH

Prior to the setting up of the Falklands Inquiry under Lord Franks, a good deal of emphasis was placed on the practice that the Government of the day does not disclose to an outside body the papers of a previous Government without the consent of the former Prime Minister concerned. There is a related practice that the Government of the day does not itself have access to the papers of a previous Government of a different political party, although this has sometimes been questioned on the grounds that 'how can new Ministers be expected to start without full knowledge, available to their civil servants, of what has happened previously?' It may therefore be of some interest to set down what the conventions are and how they operate.

The first point to make is that they are indeed conventions (defined in the *OED* as a 'general agreement or consent as embodied in any accepted usage') and are not a matter of law. In law, all Government records—past and present—are the property of the Crown: and since the Crown acts on the advice of the Government of the day, the latter could theoretically dispose at will of the papers of a former Administration, although The Queen could well first exercise her Bagehotian right to 'counsel, encourage and warn'. The need for the conventions becomes obvious, however, when it is realized that they reconcile two otherwise potentially conflicting requirements. The first is that papers of a previous Government should be preserved to allow continuity of administration, research into the past, and eventual release to the Public Record Office: in other words, to ensure that outgoing

From *Public Law* (1982), pp. 514–18. Reprinted by permission of Stevens & Sons Limited.

Ministers do not destroy or remove any papers that might embarrass them, as they sometimes did at one time and as they still do in some other countries. The second follows from the first. It is the need to avoid new Ministers using such papers to make unfair political capital at the expense of their predecessors. Mr Foot put this well in the debate on 8 July 1982, when he said:

There is the question of rummaging in the pigeon holes and other places where the work and deliberations of previous Governments may be found . . . It would be an inhibition to good government if every incoming Administration were to spend considerable time examining what the previous Administration did, with special access to matters that the previous Administration had been most anxious to keep quiet.[1]

Hence, to quote Jennings: 'The Ministers of one Government are not entitled to examine the Cabinet documents of their predecessors, though some of these documents (without the minutes) will be in the secret departmental files.'[2] And it follows that, if present Ministers are not themselves entitled to see certain papers, they can hardly agree to their release to a third party without the consent of those whose papers they were.

The papers of the Cabinet and its Ministerial Committees are clearly in a class of their own. They are the apex of government decision-taking and by definition contain the personal views of Ministers. The convention applies to them without exception and if any question of releasing them to third parties arises, the consent of The Queen is always sought. But the convention applies equally to any minutes or other documents written by a former Minister in the course of his ministerial duties and not publicly available. Furthermore, just as the private views of their predecessors in office are not disclosed to their successors, so the advice tendered to them by officials is also not disclosed since this would reveal whether they accepted or ignored it.

How then is there any continuity of policy or any profiting from past experience?

---

[1] HC Deb., Vol. 27, col. 474.
[2] Sir I. Jennings, *Cabinet Government* (3rd edn., 1965), p. 274.

In the first place, there are three categories of papers which are generally regarded as excepted from the convention:

(i) Papers which, even if not publicly available, can be deemed to be in the public domain, e.g. letters sent by former Ministers to trade associations, trade unions, etc., or to Members of Parliament about constituency cases, or to members of the public.

(ii) Papers, other than genuinely personal messages, dealing with matters which are known to foreign governments, e.g. messages about inter-governmental negotiations.

(iii) Written Opinions of the Law Officers, which are essentially legal rather than political documents.

Papers in all three categories may, if necessary in the interests of continuity, be shown to succeeding administrations. That does, however, leave a large area where the national interest requires some continuity of policy (or at least knowledge of what has happened before) and where it would be unreasonable to expect new Ministers to start with a clean sheet.

There is a clear enough principle to apply—namely, to provide new Ministers with all the information they need without politically embarrassing former Ministers—but there is no neat formula other than common sense for applying it. Clearly there is no difficulty in giving a new Minister a general account of previous policy, including the reasons for it, in a particular field. It is another matter to let him examine the personal observations of his predecessor. There will be some papers which can be shown to a new Minister without embarrassment, even though his predecessor may also have seen them: these could include reports by officials which contain no indication of the advice given to or the views expressed by the previous Minister. In other cases, a Minister may need factual information which is contained in a document prepared for his predecessor, but his predecessor may have been personally involved or expressed views on paper. In such cases, the requirement can often be met by preparing a self-contained memorandum setting out all the salient facts without attaching papers disclosing the advice given to the previous Minister or his observations on it. The topic involved may also have a bearing on the documents that can be shown to a new Minister. Foreign policy is the classic example of a field where continuity of knowledge is important. So are papers dealing with individual cases, though even with them there is sometimes a political content which would make it inappropriate to show a new Minister the personal views of his predecessor on the handling of an individual case. Normally common sense will show clearly enough how to reconcile the general principle of the convention with the practical needs of continuity, and in practice the operation of the convention gives rise to very few difficulties. In cases of genuine doubt, or if for example it is felt that papers disclosing the comments or views of a previous Minister ought to be disclosed to his successor, then the normal practice would be to consult the former Minister.

Conventions are not of course static. An alternative definition to the *OED* one quoted above would be 'the sum of the precedents'. For example, the conventions arose from the need to preserve ministerial papers and to protect them from exploitation by a subsequent Government of a different political complexion. The statement made by the then Prime Minister at the time when a further inquiry into the circumstances dealt with in the Bingham Report was being considered, and the discussions when the setting up of the Falklands Inquiry was being debated, make it clear that, if what is at issue is disclosure to a third party, then the consent of the former Prime Minister or Minister concerned should be sought, even though he may be of the same political party as the current Administration. To that extent, the conventions have over the course of time been made rather more precise, even though they have not changed.

Since, as I say, the conventions are neither a matter of law nor static, no formal or exact definition of them exists. A careful reading of the debate in the House of Commons on 8 July and other publicly available sources suggests that a current formulation would be as follows:

(i) Current Ministers may not see the Cabinet papers of former Ministers of a different political party. Nor may they see other papers (except in a few well-defined

categories) giving the unpublished views or comments
of their predecessors or the advice submitted to them.

(ii) Current Ministers may normally see the papers of
former Ministers of the same political party provided
the need to do so arises in the course of their current
ministerial duties. There could be exceptional circumstances in which it might be appropriate first to
seek the agreement of the former Prime Minister
concerned.

(iii) Before affording access to the Cabinet papers or other
ministerial documents of a previous Government
(whether of the same political party or not) to anyone
not otherwise entitled to see them, the current Prime
Minister would seek the agreement of the former
Prime Minister concerned or, if he were not available,
the current leader of his party.

Furthermore, since documents of a previous Administration
are retained in Government departments subject to these
conventions, it follows that:

(a) Former Ministers may have access to, but not retain,
any documents which they saw when in office;

(b) officials have a duty to provide present Ministers with
all relevant information about departmental policy or
past events subject to not disclosing the personal views
or comments of previous Ministers or the advice
submitted directly to them.

10

MINISTERS AND THE ATTORNEY-GENERAL

J. LL. J. EDWARDS

The tradition of independence is of considerable antiquity though there have been times when it has not enjoyed the same level of universal recognition claimed for it in 1959. Lord Eldon expressed the same philosophy in equally trenchant language in 1793,[1] and in 1903 we find Prime Minister A. J. Balfour adhering to the same principles in stating:

It is due to the Attorney General to say in the clearest manner, not only in the interests of the Attorney General but in the interest of all, that his position as the Director of Public Prosecutions [*sic*] is a position absolutely independent of any of his colleagues. It is not in the power of the Government to direct the Attorney General to direct a prosecution. No government would do such thing; no Attorney General would tolerate its being done.[2]

Further corroboration of the acceptance of this doctrine and of the need to maintain a separation of functions between the Government and the Law Officers in decisions affecting prosecutions is to be found in the parliamentary statements of Mr Gladstone in 1873[3] and Lord Salisbury in 1896.[4] At the

From *The Attorney General, Politics and the Public Interest*, pp. 318, 319 (1984). Reprinted by permission of Sweet and Maxwell Limited.

[1] Twiss, *The Public and Private Life of Lord Chancellor Eldon* (3rd edn., 1846) i. 158, quoted in J. Ll. J. Edwards, *The Law Officers of the Crown* (1964), p. 179.

[2] The Prime Minister was speaking at the close of the debate on a motion expressing regret that no prosecution had been instituted against the directors of the London & Globe Finance Corporation, among whom was the notorious financier, Whittaker Wright. Parl. Deb., Vol. 118, ser. 4, cols. 349–80. 19 Feb. 1903. Balfour's remarks are reported ibid. col. 376–7. See, too, the speech of Sir Robert Finlay, the Attorney-General, ibid. cols. 359–61.

[3] Parl. Deb., HC, Vol. 216, ser. 3, cols. 1064–5 and see Edwards, op. cit., pp. 184–5. The circumstances which occasioned Gladstone's remarks were the allegedly contemptuous comments on the *Tichborne* case made by several members of the House of Commons.

[4] Parl. Deb., HL, Vol. 42, col. 519, 2 July 1896. In issue was the question whether

time they made these pronouncements each as occupying the position of Prime Minister. And reference has already been made to the important distinction drawn by Prime Minister Baldwin in 1924 between, on the one hand, the Attorney-General's duty to inform himself of all relevant circumstances which might properly affect his decision including the views of the Government or of the appropriate Minister and, on the other hand, the rejection of the edict adopted by Ramsay MacDonald's administration to the effect that no prosecution of a political character should be undertaken without the prior sanction of the Cabinet having been first obtained.[5]

THE SHAWCROSS STATEMENT IN 1951

In more modern times the classic pronouncement on the role of the Attorney-General in exercising his prerogative and statutory responsibilities is that contained in Sir Hartley Shawcross's speech in 1951 in the House of Commons when explaining his decision to prosecute in the *Gas Strikers* case.[6] It deserves repetition:

The true doctrine is that it is the duty of the Attorney General, in deciding whether to not to authorise the prosecution, to acquaint himself with all the relevant facts, including, for instance, the effect which the prosecution, successful or unsuccessful as the case may be, would have upon public morale and order, and with any other consideration affecting public policy. In order so to inform himself, he may, although I do not think he is obliged to, consult with any of his colleagues in the government, and indeed, as Lord Simon once said, he would in some cases be a fool if he did not. On the other hand, the assistance of his colleagues is confined to informing him of particular considerations which might affect his own decision, and does not consist, and must not consist, in telling him what that decision ought to be. The responsibility for the eventual decision rests with the Attorney General, and he is not to be put, and is

the Attorney-General, Sir Richard Webster, when demanding a trial at bar in the *Jameson Raid* case, was acting on his own absolute discretion or under the orders of the Government. For the views of Lord Halsbury LC, see ibid, col. 517, and Lord Herschell, see ibid. col. 518. As to this episode and for an examination of Herschell's experience as a Law Officer, see Edwards, op. cit., pp. 186–7.

[5] See the general treatment of this subject in Edwards, op. cit. pp. 212–25.

[6] For the background to this case see Edwards, op. cit., pp. 220–3.

not put, under pressure by his colleagues in the matter. Nor, of course, can the Attorney General shift his responsibility for making the decision on to the shoulders of his colleagues. If political considerations which in the broad sense that I have indicated affect government in the abstract arise it is the Attorney General, applying his judicial mind, who has to be the sole judge of those considerations.[7]

This carefully phrased exposition of the proper approach to be followed by the Attorney-General, when faced with a situation in which questions of national or international public policy may surround the exercise of his prosecutorial discretion, was the result of a collaborative effort that serves further to underline the major importance which has been accorded to Shawcross's statement in the intervening years. For, as the files in the Law Officers' Department reveal, the Attorney-General went to infinite pains to ensure, as he put it, 'that the integrity of the office should be very fully maintained since its position is, I am afraid, often widely misunderstood'.[8] Among the individuals to whom draft copies of Shawcross's proposed statement had previously been circulated for comment were Viscount Simon, Viscount Jowitt, and Lord Kilmuir, each of them a former Law Officer of the Crown who subsequently rose to become Lord Chancellor. In addition, Shawcross sought the views of Sir Theobald Mathew, the Director of Public Prosecutions, and Mr Herbert Morrison, the Lord President of the Council and Deputy Prime Minister.

[7] HC Deb., Vol. 483, cols. 683–4, 29 Jan. 1951. In the course of his comprehensive exposition of the Attorney-General's responsibility for prosecutions (ibid. cols. 679–90) Shawcross also stated that in deciding whether or not to prosecute in a particular case 'there is only one consideration which is altogether excluded and that is the repercussion of a given decision upon my personal or my party's or the government's political fortunes: that is a consideration which never enters into account'—ibid. col. 682.

[8] In a letter from Shawcross to Viscount Simon, Dec. 1950—LOD (Law Officers' Dept.) files.

11

THE WESTLAND AFFAIR

PETER HENNESSY

When Mrs Margaret Thatcher dies and the pathologists try to discover what made this remarkable woman tick they will find a little helicopter engraved on her heart. Westland is for Mrs Thatcher what Calais was for Mary Tudor for all her determined efforts to dismiss it (and the attempted sale of Land Rover to General Motors shortly after) as 'comparatively small things . . . if I may say so, very small things'. The affair was breathtaking not because of the issue involved—Westland *was* a small aircraft company in the west country of which the political nation knew little—but because of the brilliant shaft of light it projected on Mrs Thatcher's Whitehall which threw familiar landmarks into sharp, surprising, and alarming relief. Westland reduced old constitutional nostrums to rubble. One veteran observer, Professor John Griffith of the London School of Economics, offered a new definition worthy of Bagehot at his tersest: 'The constitution', he said, 'is what happens'.

The Westland affair was a drama in seven parts:

(1) Autumn 1984–Summer 1985. Routine industrial rescue case handled at interdepartmental level in Whitehall.

(2) Summer–Autumn 1985. Collective decisions taken at ministerial level.

(3) Late November–mid-December 1985. Issue becomes controversial within the machine as rival Ministers and departments line up behind rival rescue schemes.

(4) Mid-December 1985–early January 1986. Westland develops into an issue of Cabinet procedure.
and

(5) The private debate goes public as rival departments

From *Journal of Law and Society*, 13 (1986), 423–32. © Basil Blackwell. Reprinted with permission.

brief and counterbrief the Press and back-bench MPs.

(6) On 9 January 1986 the issue explodes politically when Mr Michael Heseltine, Secretary of State for Defence, walks out of a Cabinet meeting and resigns.

(7) Protracted aftermath as issue becomes a staple of party strife, embedded in select Committee inquiries and enters political folklore as a *cause célèbre*.

The opening phase of Westland was as dispiriting as it was familiar as part of what Peter Riddell has called 'the case-work of decline'. Yet another British industry was on the ropes and appealing for Government succour. In the autumn of 1984 Westland's financial position 'began to give cause for concern' at the Department of Trade and Industry and the Ministry of Defence. By the summer of 1985 Westland was creeping up the Whitehall agenda. On 18 and 19 June a group of Ministers met under Mrs Thatcher's chairmanship to consider the use of public funds to bail out the company. Despite its importance as a defence contractor, Westland's salvation was to be left to the market. At the end of June Westland's directors approached the Bank of England for advice. Through the Bank's good offices, Sir John Cuckney, a seasoned company doctor and specialist in ailing firms, became chairman of Westland on 26 June. Early in July Westland informed Whitehall that the United Technologies Corporation, which encompasses the American helicopter manufacturer Sikorsky, was interested in 'some form of participation' in Westland. On 2 September Mr Leon Brittan was appointed Secretary of State for Trade and Industry. The dramatis personae of the Westland affair were in place.

By the end of September Westland's preference for a partnership with Sikorsky had been conveyed to the Government as part of Cuckney's plans for a financial reconstruction of the company. On 4 October Leon Brittan sent a minute to the Prime Minister on Westland's future noting that Sikorsky was the most likely candidate for taking a minority share-holding, adding that the company should, none the less, be encouraged to pursue the possibility of a European solution. On 16 October, rather late in the day, Michael Heseltine emerged as the champion of a European partnership at a meeting of Ministers chaired by Mr Brittan. As a result, Heseltine was authorized, as the Prime Minister later put it, to 'explore further the possibility of an alternative association with Aerospatiale, MBB and Agusta becoming available for consideration by the Board of Westland'.

Heseltine, who likes to turn any ministry he occupies into a miniature Department of Industry, applied his formidable enthusiasm and energy to a case that combined two of his greatest passions—the preservation of a strong manufacturing base in Britain and closer European collaboration. As Westland rose up the Government's agenda so did the political temperature inside Whitehall, though, at this stage, the thermometers of the political, defence, and industrial journalists failed to detect it. On 27 November Mr Heseltine had a meeting with his West German counterpart Dr Manfred Woerner. As a result a meeting of the national armaments directors of the British, West German, French, and Italian governments was fixed for 29 November in London. The directors took the Heseltine line and recommended to their governments 'that the needs of their Forces within the 3 classes [13 tonne, 8–9 tonne and Light Attack Helicopter] should be covered solely in the future by helicopters designed and built in Britain'.

That meeting on 29 November put Westland into political orbit. Leon Brittan was goaded by Heseltine's 'enthusiasm for a European solution to this problem [which] had caused him to take action going beyond what was consistent with the Government's policy in relation to the handling of Westland'. From now on the usual channels of Whitehall policy-making were infected by a poison and a personal animus which were eventually to cost both Heseltine and Brittan their Cabinet jobs. The Ministry of Defence was lined up against the Department of Trade and Industry. At such times Whitehall has a genius for applying the oil-can in the shape of a Cabinet committee in which the protagonists are separated then reconciled. On this occasion, the forum for managing conflict was not a formal Cabinet committee but one of those informal *ad hoc* groups in which the Prime Minister prefers to do business. She has a tendency to stack the membership of such groups to secure the result she wants. Heseltine had been a victim of this tactic in September 1981 when, as Environment Secretary, he had proposed an ambitious programme of inner city regeneration in the aftermath of that summer's urban riots.

The Prime Minister's Westland group met on 5 and 6 December. Present in addition to Heseltine, Brittan, and herself were Sir Geoffrey Howe, Foreign Secretary, John MacGregor, Chief Secretary to the Treasury, and Sir Patrick Mayhew, Solicitor-General. The meetings were rancorous in tone. 'One hostile critic' was quoted in *The Observer* as saying 'she ranted and raved. It was typical of the way she conducts Cabinet Government'. The Prime Minister's support for the Brittan–Cuckney view of Sikorsky as preferred saviour is not disputed. The outcome of those meetings is. In his resignation statement Heseltine claimed that the Prime Minister failed to achieve her objective which was to 'close-off the European option' for the Westland rescue. By the following Monday 'Downing Street sources' were telling journalists that the records of those two *ad hoc* meetings showed 'that a majority of those present were probably prepared to repudiate or reject' the course proposed by the national armaments directors. A source close to Heseltine quickly countered with 'That is a lie'. On 15 Janaury 1986 Mrs Thatcher gave her version to the Commons:

At the end of the second meeting on 6 December it was clear that a majority of the Ministers present were ready to decide that the Government should reject the recommendation from the National Armaments Directors, thus leaving Westland free to reach its own decision. But because a minority of Ministers—including my Rt. Hon friend the member for Henley [Heseltine]—felt very strongly about the matter, I decided that a further discussion must be held in Cabinet Committee, namely in the Economic Sub-Committee, for which a full paper should be prepared.

Westland had, at last, flown into the formal structure of Cabinet government where, according to the tradition lovingly promulgated by Prime Ministers of all political hues, the doctrine of collective responsibility asserts the magic that holds administrations together. At the meeting of EA (Cabinet Office code for the Economic Committee) on 9 December the magic failed to work. The row over what transpired was to fuel the grievance which eventually propelled Michael Heseltine from the Cabinet Room. That meeting has become a *locus classicus* for students of the British constitution, political pathologists worried by the health of the Cabinet system, and observers of the Thatcher style.

Apart from anything else the attendance list was highly unorthodox as two outsiders, neither of whom was bound by the Privy Counsellor's oath of confidentiality, were present— Sir John Cuckney and Mr Marcus Agius, a director of Lazard's, Westland's financial advisers. Mrs Thatcher later explained their presence in a Commons statement. They were 'invited to attend for part of the time to report on their company's position and to answer questions'. EA concluded, in Mrs Thatcher's words:

. . . that, unless a viable European package which the Board of Westland could recommend to its shareholders was in place by 4.00 pm on 13 December—Friday of that week—the Government would make it clear that the country would not be bound by the recommendation of the national armaments directors.

The controversy surrounding the outcome of EA on 9 December was stirred by contradictory interpretations of the *procedure* it was or was not agreed to follow from that point. For Mr Heseltine the position was translucent:

The meeting ended with a clear statement that we would meet again on Friday at 3.00 pm when the Stock Exchange closed. The officials of the Cabinet Office recorded the words. They are not in the minutes but I believe them to be in the notebooks from which the minutes are prepared. It was no surprise to me when, therefore, the Cabinet Office arranged the meeting for Friday at 3 o'clock. It was a devastating surprise when it subsequently cancelled the meeting.

Mrs Thatcher's memory is very different from Heseltine's:

It was recognised in discussion [on 9 December] that the timetable would allow for another meeting of Ministers before 4.00 pm on 13 December if unforeseen developments required one, but no decision to hold such a meeting was taken or recorded. The conclusion was clear, the events happened and the decision took effect. No meeting was agreed, so there was no meeting to cancel . . . in the light of the decisions taken on 9 December there was no further issue to discuss.

It was on this difference of interpretations about the next step agreed at EA on 9 December that the Heseltine resignation turned as he made plain in an interview with me in April 1986:

HENNESSY: What was it you objected to about the conduct of *ad hoc* meetings, the economic strategy committee, etc., and a meeting that didn't take place, that led you to make very serious allegations in public over a fortnight?

HESELTINE: Well, I've nothing against *ad hoc* committees. It's often the most efficient way of running government, and every Prime Minister who does it should do it if you can get agreement of the people principally involved, then it's a sensible way to conduct affairs, and I've nothing to say against that at all.

I've got nothing against the procedures which led to the Economic Affairs Committee on the Monday in early December. It was a perfectly proper decision for the Prime Minister to take in order to reach agreement on a matter that was controversial when put to small groups of Ministers. Indeed, it was the right procedure—tried to get a decision in small groups, wasn't able to get it, took it to a properly constituted committee of the Cabinet. Absolutely the right way to behave. My complaint is a very narrow but fundamental complaint, that at that properly constituted economic committee of the Cabinet, it was agreed that I would be given five days to . . . bring flesh and blood to a European option.

And the properly constituted Cabinet committee would meet on the Friday, at the end of the week, in order to make a judgment about what I'd done, because otherwise there was no point in giving me the opportunity, because it was going to be a Ministerial approach I was going to adopt. I wasn't off to do something in a sort of commercial sense. I was going to talk to Ministers and other governments. So of course the British government had to look to see what I'd been able to achieve in dialogue with my European Ministerial colleagues, make a judgment about it and in the meeting that took place on the Monday, the Prime Minister clearly said there would be a meeting on the Friday at 3 o'clock when the Stock Exchange closed so I was content. And that meeting was arranged on the Tuesday, in advance of the Friday; it was cancelled on the Wednesday.

And that was the point at which I was never to get a chance for my Ministerial consultations with Europe to be exposed to my Cabinet colleagues for their collective judgment. So the majority that had supported me on the Monday were never going to be allowed to reconvene on the Friday.

That was a break in trust between myself and the Prime Minister and if that breach of trust was to lead to a decision that Westland was to move under effective American control, I wasn't prepared to go along with that technique of governing this country. What could be done once like that to a Secretary of State for Defence could be done again, and I wouldn't be prepared to be in that position.

HENNESSY: By cancelling that meeting, do you think the PM cheated?

HESELTINE: I think that is a breakdown of trust between the Prime Minister and the Secretary of State for Defence. I think it is constitutionally unacceptable, and I said so at the time. I made quite clear that if it was persisted with, then I would leave the Cabinet. And that was known for some five weeks. And in the end it was persisted with and I left.

HENNESSY: You're saying the PM bent the rules.

HESELTINE: Well I've described it in my own words, and I think that's clear enough.

HENNESSY: What happened at full Cabinet where you raised the issue?

HESELTINE: Subsequently? Well there was never a discussion of the substantive issue after that.

HENNESSY: There was the fact that your dissent was not minuted.

HESELTINE: Well that was all part of the process which built from the moment on of cancelling that meeting that was going to take place on the Friday, cancelling it on the Wednesday, then a whole range of things happened, which are all publicly documented, in order to . . . ensure that what I believe invalid decision—had a chance of success. It would never have had a chance of success without all those things happening.

The argument about the cancelled meeting still rages. The Commons Defence Committee sympathizes with Michael Heseltine: 'It is . . . remarkable that having been given this commission by his colleagues, Mr Heseltine was allowed no opportunity to report formally to those colleagues.' Mr Leon Brittan, the other ministerial victim of Westland, does not: 'There was no cheating of any kind—that's a ridiculous suggestion.'

The cancellation of the 13 December meeting began the process that was to lead to a constitutional meltdown. On 19 December at a meeting of the full Cabinet Heseltine, as he said later, 'again asked for collective judgment. It was again denied me.' By the time the Cabinet met on 19 December

Heseltine had begun to take his case to the public. Initially he appeared to have been licensed to do so. On 17 December Downing Street sources told political correspondents the Prime Minister believed his activities to be 'unorthodox but in order'. But after the Cabinet meeting on 19 December those same sources let it be known that Heseltine had been rebuffed in Cabinet for puncturing the collective line.

By Christmas week both Mr Heseltine and Mrs Thatcher had sinned against constitutional convention. By going public Heseltine had flouted *Questions of Procedure for Ministers*, the Cabinet's bible of dos and don'ts. He had driven a coach and horses through its section on collective responsibility which reads:

Decisions reached by the Cabinet or Cabinet Committee are normally announced and defended by the Minister concerned as his own decisions. There may be rare occasions when it is desirable to emphasise the importance of some decision by stating specifically that it is the decision of Her Majesty's Government. This, however, should be the exception rather than the rule. The growth of any general practice whereby decisions of the Cabinet or of Cabinet Committees were announced as such would lead to the embarrassing result that some decisions of Government would be regarded as less authoritative than others. Critics of a decision reached by a particular Committee could press for its review by some other Committee or by the Cabinet, and the constitutional right of individual Ministers to speak in the name of the Government as a whole would be impaired.

Heseltine had spared no effort in making the government line on Westland appear 'less authoritative than others' and was vigorously pressing for a review.

There are no written rules covering the right of a dissenting Minister to take an issue to full Cabinet. But the normal conventions were explained by Lord Hunt of Tanworth, Secretary of the Cabinet 1973–9:

HENNESSY: How about Cabinet Ministers having a right to put an issue onto the agenda of full Cabinet, that's been controversial in the Westland affair as well, what's your understanding of the constitutional practice there?
HUNT: The constitutional practice is that the agenda is produced by the Secretary of the Cabinet and approved by the Prime Minister.

Any minister can ask for an item to go on in the ordinary way his department will have asked. And if it is the right time for it to come to Cabinet, if there is room on the agenda, it'll be on. But if a minister is unsatisfied and wants an item included which isn't on, he can always ask. And I've known that happen, and in the ordinary way the Prime Minister will agree.

HENNESSY: But Prime Ministers have the right to keep things off the agenda if they want to, for whatever reason?

HUNT: I have never known a Prime Minister keep an item off an agenda for what one might call a disreputable or tactical reason. I mean there have been times where I've known a Prime Minister say, we have ten items next week, there simply isn't time, or it is not the right time to discuss this because . . . But where you've had a position of a minister who is unhappy and unsatisfied that an issue is not being given a hearing, I've never known a Prime Minister refuse to have it on the agenda.

Under the parameters outlined by Lord Hunt, Heseltine should have had his full Cabinet discussion. He was a political heavyweight and, with Brittan, one of the two lead Ministers on the Westland issue. He had reason to be aggrieved.

So did Mrs Thatcher and Mr Brittan. Over the Christmas period Michael Heseltine won the battle of the headlines. In planning their counterstroke the Thatcher–Brittan camp turned a crisis into a catastrophe, assaulted a third constitutional convention—ministerial responsibility for the actions of their civil servants—and reopened a growing concern in the mid-1980s with the ethical position of officials instructed to act in an improper manner by their political superiors. Again the value of the Select Committee system is demonstrated by the Commons Defence Committee's careful reconstruction of events between Saturday, 4 January and Monday, 6 January 1986.

The chief weapon of the Whitehall war over Westland was the non-attributable briefing to the Press. The Ministry of Defence and the Department of Trade and Industry used it systematically. Downing Street has a press machine which provides a daily service on this basis—the controversial lobby system—which it could deploy on Westland duties at will. In late December and early January combat by competitive letter took to the field of battle. As part of this process, Mr Heseltine wrote to Mr Horne of Lloyds Merchant Bank, an adviser to the European Consortium seeking to rescue

Westland, including material the Ministry of Defence had wanted inserted into an earlier letter from Mrs Thatcher to Sir John Cuckney. It had been rejected. As the Defence Committee report indicated, Heseltine's note to Horne raised the temperature to boiling-point commenting that 'the effect of such a letter upon the Prime Minister and the Secretary of State for Trade can have been nothing short of incendiary'.

The Heseltine letter led to a weekend of feverish activity in No. 10 and the DTI. Mrs Thatcher read the exchanges between Horne and Heseltine on Saturday, 4 January. Realizing Heseltine's reply had not been cleared by the Government's Law Officers she sent a message to Brittan suggesting that he 'as the sponsoring Minister for Westlands . . . should ask the Solicitor-General to consider . . . the Defence Secretary's letter and give his opinion on whether it was accurate and consistent with my own letter to Sir John Cuckney'. By mid-morning on Monday, 6 January Sir Patrick Mayhew, the Solicitor-General, had completed his letter. By mid-afternoon Miss Colette Bowe, Brittan's Head of Information at DTI, though troubled about the propriety of her action, had leaked selectively parts of the Mayhew letter most damaging to Heseltine to Chris Moncrieff of the Press Association on Brittan's instructions after obtaining 'cover' from Bernard Ingham, the Prime Minister's Chief Press Secretary, and Mr Charles Powell, the Downing Street private secretary specializing in foreign and defence matters.

Miss Bowe's leak backfired more damagingly than any Whitehall press operation in recent memory. It produced an instant parliamentary furore, a farcical leak inquiry by Sir Robert Armstrong, the Cabinet Secretary (the Law Officers may well have resigned if the leak inquiry had not been set in motion), it re-fuelled an existing Select Committee inquiry and started a second. Controversy raged for months and, even with Parliament in summer recess at the time of writing (August 1986), the suspicion remains that Westland is hissing like 'an unexploded bomb' beneath Mrs Thatcher's Downing Street. The details of the Westland affair from the time of the Bowe leak do not need to be reprised here. But the constitutional implications of the manner of the subsequent inquests and their outcome do merit a serious look.

The standard constitutional view of the role of civil servants and Ministers is as familiar as it is banal: civil servants are accountable to Ministers, Ministers are accountable to Parliament. This simple chain had already been broken routinely by Select Committee inquiries when MPs, at public hearings, had questioned named officials about individual items of policy on which they had advised Ministers. The officials never disclosed that advice, but they became personally associated with areas of departmental activity. Westland, according to a former permanent secretary, moved civil servants from a difficult position into 'an impossible position'. For a start, said the aggrieved retired official, it was the Prime Minister herself who had named the five civil servants involved in the leaking of the Mayhew Letter during her Commons statement on the result of the Cabinet Secretary's leak inquiry. Mr Brittan, had, in the end, accepted ministerial responsibility for his officials' actions and resigned. The Prime Minister had not. And Ministers had prevented the five named officials from defending themselves before the Commons Defence Committee. For this particular seasoned public servant, Westland had changed the constitutional landscape beyond recognition. No official in future would know where she or he stood.

By a nice irony of timing, the Government published its reply to the Treasury and Civil Service Committee's report on the duties and responsibilities of civil servants on the same day that the Defence Committee released its outspoken criticisms of 'improper' ministerial and official behaviour over Westland. Its section on accountability was worded as if Westland had never happened:

The Government endorses the Committee's two basic propositions on accountability: that ministers and not officials are responsible and accountable for policy; and that officials' advice to Ministers is and should remain confidential. Constitutionally, Ministers are responsible and accountable for all actions carried out by civil servants of their departments in pursuit of Government policies or in the discharge of responsibilities laid upon them by Parliament.

Despite the grand constitutional language in which much of the Westland debate has been couched inside Parliament and out, it was raw politics and not matters of convention or probity that prevailed throughout. Managing a difficult colleague, not *Questions of Procedure for Ministers*, determined Mrs Thatcher's initial decision to let Michael Heseltine to go rogue and prepare a European alternative to Sikorsky. Damage limitation and not the imperatives of collective responsibility lay behind her efforts to rein him in during mid-December. Assertion of her political supremacy explains her determination to foreclose discussion after the EA meeting of 9 December. The need to turn the tide in the battle for public opinion led (by whatever route history may eventually uncover) to the leaking of the Solicitor-General's letter on 6 January.

It was the Prime Minister's attempt to gag Heseltine by insisting at the Cabinet meeting of 9 January that in future he clear all his statements on Westland with the Cabinet Office which finally triggered his resignation. Pressure from Conservative back-benchers forced Leon Brittan to follow Heseltine out of the Government, not the requirements of ministerial responsibility. The need to preserve the position of the Prime Minister and not constitutional doctrine led the Conservative majority on the Commons Defence Committee to 'clear' Mrs Thatcher. Naming and blaming the civil servants involved, albeit on a sliding scale of culpability, was done without a moment's pause to consider the conventions of ministerial and official responsibility. 'Procedure', in Sir Kenneth Pickthorn's famous phrase, may be 'all the Constitution the poor Briton has'. But in the Westland affair it provided not one jot of protection or guidance for the system or the people who work in it. The constitution really was reduced to what happened.

PART III

INDIVIDUAL RESPONSIBILITY

12

PRIME MINISTERIAL
ANSWERABILITY

HAROLD WILSON

Prime Ministers approach the bi-weekly ordeal by questions in different frames of mind, but of two things I am sure: no Prime Minister looks forward to 'PQs' with anything but apprehension; every Prime Minister works long into the night on his answers, and on all the notes available to help him anticipate the instant and unpredictable supplementary questions that follow his main prepared answer.

It has been said that Harold Macmillan, a highly successful performer at Question Time, used on occasion to be physically sick, or very near to it, before Questions on Tuesdays and Thursdays. In my address to the British Academy I said that, if Britain ever had a Prime Minister who did not fear questions, our parliamentary democracy would be in danger.

In seven years eight months as Prime Minister I answered more than 12,000 parliamentary questions, oral or written, the figure for 1974–5 reaching over 2000.

The questions are tabled to the Prime Minister, as to other Ministers, well in advance. There used to be a three-week limit on the period ahead for which a question could be tabled; in earlier days, an unlimited period could mean that an MP who wanted to be sure of an oral answer by getting high on the list would table his question many weeks in advance. This led to complaints that questions tabled in a given situation, even a crisis situation, were long out of date when the relevant Ministers came to answer them orally. Even the three-week period led to questions that were very *passées*, so a fortnight's limit was laid down. With the speed of events in modern Britain, even this limit fails to prevent time

From *The Governance of Britain* (1976). Reprinted by permission of Weidenfeld and Nicolson Ltd.

being taken on issues which, while relevant, perhaps sensation-
alized at the time of their tabling, appear archaic by the time
they are answered. A fortnight is a long time in politics.

With Prime Minister's Questions—and some others—there
is a rush to table as soon as the Order Paper of the House is
open to them. As soon as the Prime Minister sits down, on a
Tuesday or Thursday, after answering the last of the
questions on the Order Paper for that day, the Table Office is
handling the questions. Some are handed in at that moment;
some have been handed in and are awaiting attention
preparatory to being placed on the order Paper; some have
been sent in by post. The modern practice is to assemble them
all together at 4.00 p.m. and send them to the printer, without
first arranging them in any set order, to establish pride of
place on the Order Paper. The actual 'lottery', without fear or
favour to any Hon. Member, is done by the printers.

There is a fundamental difference between Prime Minister's
Questions and those of departmental Ministers. For one
thing, most departmental Ministers face questions only once
every three, four, or five weeks, and they can divide the
questions for answering between the whole departmental
team, no doubt reflecting the devolution of duties within the
department. The Prime Minister has no Minister of State or
parliamentary Under-Secretary (except that questions put to
him in his capacity as Minister for the Civil Service are
normally handled on his behalf by the Minister of State, Civil
Service Department). But the main difference is the extremely
wide, indeed totally open-ended, nature of the supplementaries,
which can follow the main, usually stylized, question.

Supplementary questions to departmental Ministers usually
reflect their daily work, and they have a large department
ready to brief them on likely supplementaries. Their services
are, of course, available to No. 10—reams of it, attached to
the late-night briefing on the eve of Questions.

There are certain standard questions regularly put to the
Prime Minister. One of the most familiar—certainly one of
the most open-ended—is when a Member asks whether, and
when, the Prime Minister intends to pay a visit to his
constituency or some other place at home or abroad. In order
to deal with any possible supplementary the Prime Minister

has pages upon pages of briefing for each proposed visit, since the supplementary is virtually unpredictable, unless a friendly MP sends a message through the Prime Minister's PPS indicating what he is going to ask. This happens more often on the government side, though there are Opposition Members who are more interested in getting a meaningful reply on a matter of constituency interest than in scoring an extremely short-lived political point.

The range of possible supplementaries to a 'visits' question is almost unlimited. First, there are the constituency questions proper. An Hon. Member, whether from the majority or the minority side, on being told that the Prime Minister *does* plan or 'has no plans' to visit the constituency, many raise some local grievance, such as the delay in placing the promised hospital or school on the relevant department's building programme, the numbers unemployed, prospects for school-leavers, local racial problems, housing, education, the road programme, the long-delayed building of the bridge across a river, or the inadequacy of remand accommodation. The list of possible questions approaches the infinite, and almost all of them fall within the responsibility of departmental Ministers— but the Prime Minister has to be briefed and ready, and it is the duty of the No. 10 machine to see that the necessary information is there.

The second group is based on questions designed to open up policy matters, usually on a national or international issue. So when the Prime Minister has indicated his intentions on the prospects of a visit, the questioner's supplementary presses him to come to hear the views of his constituents on any single subject under the sun, from the imbalance between Soviet and NATO naval forces in the Atlantic to a speech by a trade union leader representing a minority in the TUC on the question of inflation. Again, the range of potential questions is virtually infinite, and covers not only the whole of Government responsibility but every conceivable area of national and international life.

The third group is based on invitations pressing the Prime Minister to visit not the questioner's constituency but that of another Member, very often, if the questioner is on the Opposition benches, a Member of the Government party.

When Clay Cross was in the news over the default of local councillors in relation to the previous Government's rent legislation, Conservative Members who might not have heard of Clay Cross three or four years earlier were avid for the Prime Minister's attendance there—or at least to bring him within range of questions on the said councillors. Another type of area where the Prime Minister is encouraged to put in an appearance is a town where some conference has been held, or even a speech made, not necessarily by a Minister; the supplementary will raise one of the many issues opened up, or touched on, in the speech.

A fourth group, again referring to a journey to a constituency other than that of the questioner, is to give the premier the opportunity of 'hearing the views' of someone there on any subject from agriculture to antimony. Possible supplementaries out of a proposed visit to the City of London, for example, cover a very wide area, from the system of local government there to the level of interest rates or the commodity markets, inflation, the TUC or the latest speech made by the current ministerial target figures—for much of the period in question, Tony Benn.

A fifth group of supplementaries, regardless of whether the questioner is playing at home or away, and more relevantly directed, invites the Prime Minister to see not only what people are thinking, but what they are suffering—farmers in a particular area allegedly impoverished by Government agricultural policy or EEC directives; clothing, textile, or footwear workers facing Asian or East European export competition.

On all these questions, the supplementaries will widen further and further from the original, further and further from the place indicated, until they range over the widest possible subjects, for example a speech made three thousand miles away by the Leader of the Opposition. The Prime Minister must stand his ground, produce an answer—usually greeted with cries of 'dodging, dodging', 'answer, answer', or 'resign, resign'—and hold his ground. He must meet carefully prepared supplementaries aromatic with libations of midnight oil with a spontaneous reply which he hopes is at least as good: in any case he has to survive. In the sixties, one prominent Opposition Member, now 'shadow leader of the House', told the Press he spent a few peripatetic hours every Sunday evening preparing supplementaries for the Prime Minister's Questions the following Tuesday or Thursday: in fact, over-prepared questions do not always come off.

Then there are questions asking the Prime Minister to visit likely or unlikely places abroad. Taking the visits questions in the three months from 11 December 1975 to 11 March 1976, 139 questions were tabled for oral answer about intended visits. The great majority of these were not reached, but those that were, and those that might have been, required a good deal of briefing—and estimation of what might lie behind the question.

Some were duplicated questions, with two or more Members pinpointing a place for a visit; some were repeat questions, particularly if on the first tabling the question had not been reached.

Space forbids listing all the places, but some idea of the degree of geographical interest and diversity can be gained from the fact that we had Sweden, Costa Rica, Shoreham, and Cyprus on 11 December, the North-East, Edmonton, Kirkby, the site of the proposed Scottish Assembly, Bodmin, Leyland, and Guyana on 16 December and the Isle of Wight two days later.

Early in the New Year suggestions for a Prime Ministerial progress included the Isle of Man; on 20 January we had the City of London, Leicester, Tamworth, Perth, Gloucestershire, Merseyside, Bangor (North Wales), Northern Ireland, Moscow, mid-Wales, and a tour of the Commonwealth. Late January included Dagenham, Strathavon, Iceland, China, Yugoslavia, and Portsmouth. January ended with Dodoma and NATO; 10 February covered ten places, including Helsinki, Rutland, Hong Kong, the City of London, New York, and Devil's Bridge, near Aberystwyth. Late February saw Oslo, Cleator Moor, Skelmersdale, Moscow, Glenrothes, and Zambia: on 8 March the list concludes with southern Africa, Staffordshire, the United Nations, and SHAPE.

My questioners were ingenious in discovering further ways of opening up supplementaries. If I were not going to place X, would I, with time thus saved, visit place Y? This was countered off-the-cuff, since one has no notice of supplementaries, by the reply that the question was related to visiting X, not inventing new visits out of the time saved. Mr Speaker supported this restriction. Then another one was opened up, on a question from a Scottish Nationalist about visiting Dundee. I had no plans to do so, Sir. One would not normally regard a question about Dundee, whether visited or not, as leading logically to the feats of Queen Boadicea in the first century AD, to a visit by the Chancellor of the Exchequer to St Albans, to the ruins of Verulamium, or to the qualities of the Leader of the Opposition, a lady. But the Hon. Member for St Albans asked:

If the Prime Minister goes to Dundee, will he stop off at St Albans? Will he make certain that he brings with him his right hon. Friend, the Chancellor of the Exchequer, shows him the ruins of Verulamium —sacked by Queen Boadicea—and points out what the British people will do under a woman leader if they think they are over-taxed?

My answer, unfortunately of equal length, complained of the irrelevance of the question, dwelt on the sad denouement of Queen Boadicea's reign, and called on the questioner not to advise his Leader to solve the country's problems by unconstitutional methods.

It was all a long way from the very real problems of Dundee.

From then on all similar supplementaries were answered with a general statement of disinclination to go by circuitous routes to places I had already made clear I was not intending to go to anyway.

A few final and not untypical examples to show how far the supplementary, of which the Prime Minister of course has no notice, can depart from the original venue. I was asked by a Conservative Member to visit Derbyshire. The supplementary question was

Will the Prime Minsiter answer a question which is being asked in Derbyshire by those dependent on Rolls-Royce as well as in the rest of the country wherever people are concerned about defence and engineering export orders? Who gave the Government the mandate to order the cancellation of commercial contracts between private companies and overseas customers? Does streaking into Downing

Street with a minority vote empower the Prime Minister to put at risk vast sections of British industry and export orders?

And so on and so forth. This opened up the whole question of the Government's attitude to supplying naval vessels and other arms to the Chilean dictatorship, on which I had made a statement just two days before and then answered questions covering eight columns of *Hansard*. On this occasion the question was No. 4 on the Order Paper for that day; even so it was allowed to run on for some minutes beyond the normal time of 3.30 p.m., and the exchanges covered three and a half columns of *Hansard*.

Another one from the same region wanted me to repudiate a speech by Hugh Scanlon, not made in the region, and not the subject of any Government responsibility.

A suggestion that the Prime Minister should visit his own constituency of Huyton, which he did regularly, was designed to express Conservative disapproval of a statement unhelpful to them made during the February general election by the Director-General of CBI, Campbell Adamson, not a constituent of Huyton, or given to speaking there.

A suggestion that I should visit New Zealand elicited a supplementary condemning the Government's cancellation of a good-will visit to Greece, in the days of the Colonels' dictatorship.

The Prime Minister is not entirely defenceless. When asked to visit a Member's constituency to hear the strength of constituents' views on some particular governmental iniquity, I began to take refuge in a stock reply that I did not regard it as my duty to go round the country visiting constituencies whose residents clearly had no confidence in the ability of their own Member to express their views in the House. This proved something of a deterrent, except to the totally irresponsible.

Another regular ploy is to ask whether a particular speech by a member of the Cabinet or other senior Minister— speeches by junior Ministers do not quality for this type of question—represents the policy of Her Majesty's Government. This is a question hallowed by tradition, and must be treated very seriously, since it involves the whole question of collective ministerial responsibility.

13

MINISTERIAL RESIGNATIONS

D. E. AND G. BUTLER

Resignations from ministerial office are not easy to classify. A retirement on the ground of ill health may always conceal a protest or a dismissal. However, there are some cases where Ministers have unquestionably left office because they were not willing to continue to accept collective responsibility for some part of Government policy and some cases where the individual actions of Ministers have been thought impolitic or unworthy. The following list does not include resignations made necessary because of private scandals, except when the resignation became the subject of public comment. Nor does it include even the most publicized 'refusals to serve' (e.g. I. Macleod and E. Powell in 1963).

16 Sept. 03	J. Chamberlain (*Imperial preference*)
4–15 Sept. 03	C. Ritchie, Ld. Balfour of Burleigh, Ld. G. Hamilton, D. of Devonshire, A. Elliott (*Free Trade*)
6 Mar. 05	G. Wyndham (*Ireland*)
30 Mar. 14	J. Seely (*Curragh Mutiny*)
2 Aug. 14	Vt. Morley, J. Burns (*Entry into war*)
5 Aug. 14	C. Trevelyan (*Entry into war*)
19 Oct. 15	Sir E. Carson (*Conduct of War in the Balkans*)
31 Dec. 15	Sir J. Simon (*Compulsory National Service*)
3 May 16	A. Birrell (*Irish Rebellion*)
25 June 16	E. of Selborne (*Irish Policy*)
12 July 17	A. Chamberlain (*Campaign in Mesopotamia*)
8 Aug. 17	N. Chamberlain (*Ministry of National Service*)
17 Nov. 17	Ld. Cowdray (*Conduct of the Air Ministry*)
21 Jan. 18	Sir. E. Carson (*Ireland*)

From *British Political Facts*. Reprinted by permission of Macmillan, London and Basingstoke.

25 Apr.	18	Ld. Rothermere (*Air Force*)
22 Nov.	18	Ld. R. Cecil (*Welsh disestablishment*)
12 Nov.	19	J. Seely (*Role of Air Ministry*)
14 July	21	C. Addison (*Housing*)
9 Mar.	22	E. Montagu (*Turkey*)
18 Nov.	23	A. Buckley (*Abandonment of Free Trade*)
28 Aug.	27	Vt. Cecil (*Disarmament*)
19 May	30	Sir O. Mosley (*Unemployment*)
2 Mar.	31	Sir C. Trevelyan (*Education*)
6 Mar.	31	Ld. Arnold (*Free Trade*)
9 Oct.	31	G. Lloyd-George, G. Owen (*Decision to hold a General Election*)
28 Sept.	32	Sir H. Samuel, Sir A. Sinclair, Vt. Snowden, M. of Lothian, I. Foot, Sir R. Hamilton, G. White, W. Rea, Vt. Allendale (*Free Trade*)
18 Dec.	35	Sir S. Hoare (*Laval Pact*)
22 May	36	J. Thomas (*Budget leak*)
20 Feb.	38	A. Eden, Vt. Cranborne (*Negotiations with Mussolini*)
12–16 May	38	Earl Winterton, Vt. Swinton (*Strength of the Air Force*)
16 May	38	Ld. Harlech (*Partition of Palestine*)
1 Oct.	38	A. Duff Cooper (*Munich*)
21 Jan.	41	R. Boothby (*Blocked Czechoslovakian assets*)
1 Mar.	45	H. Strauss (*Treatment of Poles by Yalta Conference*)
26 May	46	Sir B. Smith (*Overwork and criticism*)
13 Nov.	47	H. Dalton (*Budget leak*)
13 Dec.	48	J. Belcher (*Lynskey Tribunal*)
16 Apr.	50	S. Evans (*Agricultural subsidies*)
23–4 Apr.	51	A. Bevan, H. Wilson, J. Freeman (*Budget proposals*)
20 July	54	Sir T. Dugdale (*Crichel Down*)
31 Oct.	56	A. Nutting (*Suez*)
5 Nov.	56	Sir E. Boyle (*Suez*)
29 Mar.	57	M. of Salisbury (*Release of Archbishop Makarios*)
6 Jan.	58	P. Thorneycroft, E. Powell, N. Birch (*Economic Policy*)

24 Nov. 58	I. Harvey (*Private scandal*)
8 Nov. 62	T. Galbraith (*Security: exonerated and given new office 5 May 63*)
5 June 63	J. Profumo (*Lying to the House of Commons*)
19 Feb. 66	C. Mayhew (*Defence estimates*)
3 July 66	F. Cousins (*Incomes policy*)
26 July 67	Miss M. Herbison (*Social Services policy*)
16 Jan. 68	E. of Longford (*Postponement of raising school-leaving age*)
5 Feb. 68	W. Howie (*Enforcement of Party discipline*)
16 Mar. 68	G. Brown (*Conduct of Government business*)
1 July 68	R. Gunter (*General dissatisfaction*)
24 Sept. 69	J. Bray (*Permission to publish*)
28 July 71	E. Taylor (*Entry into the EEC*)
17 Oct. 71	J. More (*Entry into the EEC*)
18 July 72	R. Maudling (*Poulson Inquiry*)
22 May 73	Ld. Lambton (*Private scandal*)
23 May 73	Earl Jellicoe (*Private scandal*)
25 Sept. 74	Ld. Brayley (*Inquiry into former business interests*)
17 Oct. 74	N. Buchan (*Agriculture Department policy*)
9 Apr. 75	E. Heffer (*speaking against EEC membership in House of Commons*)[1]
10 June 75	Dame J. Hart (*dissatisfaction with PM*)
21 July 75	R. Hughes (*Incomes policy*)
21 Feb. 76	Miss J. Lestor (*Education cuts*)
21 Dec. 76	R. Prentice (*Disenchantment with Government policies*)
9 Nov. 77	J. Ashton (*Government's handling of power dispute*)
20 Nov. 78	R. Cryer (*Failure to support Kirkby Cooperative firm*)
17 Jan. 79	A. Stallard (*Extra Seats for Northern Ireland*)
18 May 81	K. Speed (*Defence estimates*)[1]
21 Jan. 82	N. Fairbairn (*handling of a Scottish prosecution*)
5 Apr. 82	Ld. Carrington, H. Atkins, R. Luce (*Falklands*)

[1] Technically a dismissal, not a resignation.

8 May 82   N. Budgen (*Northern Ireland policy*)
11 Oct. 83   C. Parkinson (*Private scandal*)
9 Jan. 86   M. Heseltine (*disagreement with Prime
                 Minister*)
4 Jan. 86   L. Brittan (*disclosure of Solicitor-
                 General's letter*)

14

THE CRICHEL DOWN CASE

D. N. CHESTER

The chief dramatis personae were a piece of land some 725 acres in extent in the County of Dorset known as Crichel Down; the Minister of Agriculture (Sir Thomas Dugdale, Bt., MP); Lieutenant-Commander Marten—a local landowner who desired to purchase the land and reunite it with the family property of which some fifteen years or so earlier 328 acres of it had been part; Mr C. G. Eastwood, Commissioner of Crown Lands and until a short time before this a senior official in the Colonial Office; Mr C. H. M. Wilcox, an Under-Secretary at the Ministry of Agriculture and Fisheries; Mr H. A. R. Thomson, a partner in a firm of estate agents, who was acting as an agent for the Crown Lands Commission; the two Parliamentary Secretaries to the Ministry (Lord Carrington and Mr G. R. H. Nugent); and the MP for the area (Mr R. Crouch). The cast also included sundry officials at various levels of the Ministry or of public bodies closely associated with that department.

Act I concerns what happened to the piece of land after it was compulsorily acquired in 1937 by the Air Ministry for use as a bombing range. How it passed into the hands of the Ministry of Agriculture in 1949 (a Ministry which would not have been able to acquire it compulsorily for their purpose). It tells of the decisions that were made and how they were made about the use to which the land should be put; of how various farmers were officially promised a chance to bid for the tenancy and of how it came about that this promise was not honoured; and of how Lieutenant-Commander Marten, not being satisfied that his offer to acquire the land was being properly considered, with the help of his MP took the matter

Abridged from *Public Administration*, 32 (1954), 201–2. Reprinted by permission of Basil Blackwell Limited.

up with the Minister; and of the subsequent agitation which finally led the Minister to ask Sir Andrew Clark, QC, to enquire into the procedure adopted and report.

Act II starts with Sir Andrew's seven-day public inquiry held in Blandford, Dorset, at which almost everybody concerned (except the Minister) gave evidence. Some of the more exciting parts of the testimony were reported in all the leading newspapers and so whetted everybody's appetite for the Report (submitted to the Minister in May and published[1] a month later) and possibly stimulated a public desire for heads to fall.

The Third Act sees the initial statement by the Minister in the House of Commons on the day that the Report was published (15 June 1954). To the horror of the onlooker who knows that something dramatic is required, Sir Thomas Dugdale plays down the whole affair. The inquiry, he says, has achieved his main purpose because it has found no trace of bribery or corruption; he takes full responsibility for the actions of any officials criticized in the Report and announces that after hearing further explanations from those concerned he has formed a less unfavourable view of many of their actions. On 20 July, on that most harmless of House of Commons' motions, 'That this House do now adjourn', the Minister makes a further statement at the end of which he announces his resignation. Next day the two Parliamentary Secretaries submit their resignations, but withdraw them at the request of the Prime Minister. The position of the five officials chiefly concerned is considered by a Committee presided over by Sir John Woods (formerly Permanent Secretary to the Board of Trade), which recommends[2] that Mr Eastwood be transferred to other duties (as 'his usefulness as a public servant would be impaired if he were to remain in his present post'), and that no further action be taken in respect of the other four—in two cases because the officials

[1] Public Inquiry ordered by the Minister of Agriculture into the disposal of land at Crichel Down. Cmd. 9176.

[2] Report of a Committee appointed by the Prime Minister to consider whether certain civil servants should be transferred to other duties (Cmd. 9220). On 1 Nov. 1954 Mr Eastwood was replaced as Permanent Commissioner by Sir Osmund Cleverly (who had retired from the post in 1952) and resumed duties in the Colonial Office.

have already been transferred to other work which differs in character and needs from that of the posts in which they had been criticized. Lieutenant-Commander Marten has his costs reimbursed by the Government and is given the opportunity to purchase Crichel Down subject to the existing tenancy. Curtain.

In replying to the general debate on 20 July, the Home Secretary (not, as might have been expected, the Chancellor of the Exchequer) enlarged upon the doctrine of ministerial responsibility to meet those critics who thought that the doctrine rendered civil servants effectively responsible to no one. After pointing out that all civil servants hold their office 'at pleasure' and can be dismissed at any time by the Minister concerned, Sir David Maxwell Fyfe went on to enumerate four different categories of cases in which there may be parliamentary criticism of a Department and for which he said different considerations applied. They were:

1. Where a civil servant carries out an explicit order by a Minister, the Minister must protect the civil servant concerned.

2. Where a civil servant acts properly in accordance with the policy laid down by the Minister, the Minister must equally protect and defend him.

3. Where a civil servant 'makes a mistake or causes some delay, but not on an important issue of policy and not where a claim to individual rights is seriously involved, the Minister acknowledges the mistake and he accepts the responsibility, although he is not personally involved. He states he will take corrective action in the Department.' (col. 1290.)

4. '. . . where action has been taken by a civil servant of which the Minister disapproves and has no prior knowledge, and the conduct of the official is reprehensible, then there is no obligation on the part of the Minister to endorse what he believes to be wrong, or to defend what are clearly shown to be errors of his officers. The Minister is not bound to approve of action of which he did not know, or of which he disapproves. But, of course, he remains constitutionally responsible to Parliament for

the fact that something has gone wrong, and he alone can tell Parliament what has occurred and render an account of his stewardship.' (cols. 1290–1.)

It is interesting to see Mr Herbert Morrison's views on the subject. Mr Morrison spoke just before the Home Secretary and on this particular issue he said:

There can be no question whatever that Ministers are responsible for everything that their officers do, but if civil servants make errors or commit failures the House has a right to be assured that the Minister has dealt with the errors or failures adequately and properly, or that he will do so. That is a duty that falls on Ministers as well, and it would be wrong for a Minister automatically to defend every act of his officers or servants merely because they belong to his Department. Therefore, the House has to be satisfied that he is dealing with the matter adequately. (col. 1278.)

In his book *Government and Parliament*, published in April 1954, Mr Morrison has more to say on this point:

If a mistake is made in a Government Department the Minister is responsible even if he knew nothing about it until, for example, a letter of complaint is received from an M.P., or there is criticism in the Press, or a Question is put down for answer in the House; even if he has no real personal responsibility whatever, the Minister is still held responsible. He will no doubt criticize whoever is responsible in the Department in mild terms if it is a small mistake and in strong terms if it is a bad one, but publicly he must accept responsibility as if the act were his own. It is, however, legitimate for him to explain that something went wrong in the Department, that he accepts responsibility and apologizes for it, and that he has taken steps to see that such a thing will not happen again. (pp. 320–1.)

Later he says:

Somebody must be held responsible to Parliament and the public. It has to be the Minister, for it is he, and neither Parliament nor the public, who has official control over his civil servants. One of the fundamentals of our system of government is that some Minister of the Crown is responsible to Parliament, and through Parliament to the public, for every act of the Executive. This is a corner-stone of our system of parliamentary government. There may, however, be an occasion on which so serious a mistake has been made that the Minister must explain the circumstances and processes which resulted in the mistake, particularly if it involves an issue of civil liberty or individual rights. Now and again the House demands to know the name of the officer responsible for the occurrence. The proper answer of the Minister is that if the House wants anybody's head it must be his head as the responsible Minister, and that it must leave him to deal with the officer concerned in the Department.

There is a circumstance in which I think a considerable degree of frankness is warranted. If a Minister has given a specific order within the Department on a matter of public interest and his instructions have not been carried out, then, if he is challenged in Parliament and if he is so minded, he has a perfect right to reveal the facts and to assure the House that he has taken suitable action. Even so he must still take the responsibility. It is, I think, legitimate in such a case that disregard of an instruction should be made known, even if it involves some humiliation for the officer concerned and his colleagues knowing that he was the one who disobeyed; for the Civil Service should at all times know that the lawful orders of Ministers must be carried out. However, such a situation is rare, though I did experience one and told the House about it.

In all these matters it is well for the Minister to be forthcoming in Parliament. Unless the matter is exceptionally serious nothing is lost by an admission of error. The House of Commons is generous to a Minister who has told the truth, admitted a mistake, and apologized; but it will come down hard on a Minister who takes the line that he will defend himself and his Department whether they are right or wrong or who shuffles about evasively rather than admit that a blunder or an innocent mistake has been made. (pp. 323–4.)

What does all this add up to? In the first place it confirms the doctrine of ministerial responsibility. Civil servants, whatever their official actions, are not responsible to Parliament, but to a Minister. It is the Minister who is responsible to Parliament and it is he who must satisfy the majority in the House of Commons that he has handled a particular policy or case properly. It is for the Minister, therefore, so to direct, control, and discipline his staff that his policy and views prevail. But the fact that the Minister is responsible for everything done, or not done, by his department does not render the civil servant immune from disciplinary action or dismissal by the Minister nor even from public admonition by him in extremely serious cases, nor does it prevent the Minister from admitting to Parliament that his department is in error and reversing or modifying the decision criticised.

On the whole the House of Commons and the Press behaved with a high regard for the constitutional doctrine. In the general debate the resignation of the Minister and the recommendations of the Woods Report rather took the wind out of the sails of those who might have asked for official heads to fall. Even so there appeared to be general concern at the danger of individual civil servants being the subject of parliamentary and public discussion. But it would be useless to deny that Crichel Down has raised doubts in people's minds about the public responsibility of officials. Some must have been left with the impression that the Minister had come off pretty badly, but that little or nothing had happened to the civil servants involved. The Home Secretary's attempt to restate the doctrine of ministerial and official responsibility was hardly made on the spur of the moment and shows that the Government felt that something more was necessary than a reiteration of the simple doctrine that a Minister is responsible for all the actions of his officials.

This restatement and Mr Morrison's recent writing take account of the fact that a Minister can deal personally with only a small part of the decisions made by his department. They would appear to open up the possibility of a distinction being drawn between actions for which the Minister is responsible both to Parliament and also personally, and those for which he still remains responsible in the parliamentary sense, but which, it is known, are the fault of some official. As things stand at present, however, the latter class is likely to be very rare. A Minister appreciates that he often gains personal credit for the actions of anonymous officials and that he must take the rough with the smooth. More important, he appreciates that his political future will not be improved by appearing to be weak and having ineffective control over his department. Any Minister who tried to avoid criticism by blaming his officials would soon lose his parliamentary reputation and be felt to be an unsure Cabinet colleague.

15

ANOTHER VIEW OF CRICHEL DOWN

I. F. NICOLSON

Herbert Morrison (later Lord Morrison of Lambeth) was the last Opposition speaker, charging the Government with administrative incompetence, with succumbing to pressure by their own back-benchers 'happy that they have the scalp of a Minister', and with ceasing to put production first, but 'putting doctrinaire Tory politics first' instead. By way of introduction for the last speaker in the debate, Maxwell Fyfe, the Home Secretary, Queen's Counsel, former Law Officer, and Lord Chancellor-to-be, Morrison suggested that the fact that he was to reply to the debate was proof of the weakness of the Government's case: 'Merely because he is, or was, a distinguished lawyer, the Government perpetuates the mistake that he can, therefore, defend any rotten case of the Government.'

Maxwell Fyfe was defending himself as much as the Government as a whole, and chose to escape into empty generalities, 'three thoughts': first, sorrow for Dugdale's departure and gratitude for the magnificent way he had handled 'the problems of increasing production and harmonising guaranteed prices with a freer economy'; second, 'the prime concern of all of us', 'to see that what had taken place in regard to Crichel Down does not happen again'; and third, the need to state fairly and fully the doctrine of ministerial responsibility in regard to the Civil Service.

Maxwell Fyfe had been closely and personally associated with Crichel Down throughout the trouble, and would have done well to accept and declare his own responsibility for error, in the same manly fashion as Dugdale himself. He had,

Abridged from *The Mystery of Crichel Down* (OUP 1986), pp. 201–2. Reprinted by permission of Oxford University Press.

for instance, advised Clark's appointment (p. 120), made nonsense of the terms of reference of the inquiry (p. 166), and had had the closest connection with the affair throughout the 'collective responsibility' phase in Cabinet committee and subcommittee. What he actually said boils down to a vacuous statement that with a few exceptions civil servants hold office at pleasure and can be dismissed 'at any time' by their Minister, with an outline of the following unexhaustive categories:

  (i) Where a civil servant carries out an explicit order by a Minister, the Minister must protect him.

 (ii) Where a civil servant acts properly in accordance with the policy laid down by the Minister, the Minister must protect and defend him.

(iii) Where an official makes a mistake or causes some delay, not important or seriously involving 'a claim to individual rights' the Minister acknowledges the mistakes, accepts responsibility although not personally involved, and takes corrective action without exposing the official to public criticism.

(iv) But where action has been taken by a civil servant of which the Minister disapproves and has no prior knowledge, the Minister is not bound to defend it, but 'he remains responsible to Parliament for the fact that something has gone wrong' and 'he alone' can 'tell Parliament what has occurred and render an account of his stewardship'.

By that simplistic set of rules, the Crichel Down civil servants should have been absolutely protected under (i) and (ii), and should not have been exposed to public inquiry and criticism under (iii). And (iv), whether it applied to Crichel Down or not, is a covert admission that public inquiry was wrong: the Minister should have inquired in private—no public inquiry, no White Paper laid on the Table for debate—and, presumably, no Cabinet committees and subcommittees, merely the Minister, 'he alone' rendering to Parliament an account of his stewardship. This was not so much a set of rules as an adroit way of suggesting what was false: that no blame for Crichel Down could lie with Prime Minister and

Cabinet, but might well lie with civil servants, for actions which might not have been known to Ministers, 'indefensible' actions, in breach of individual rights, which Ministers would (of course) never have approved had they been told of them. It was the last word in the debate, and went unquestioned, both in Parliament and in the Press, becoming eventually authoritative text-book material.

16

THE INDIVIDUAL
RESPONSIBILITY OF MINISTERS

S. E. FINER

Sir Thomas Dugdale's resignation over the Crichel Down affair was widely hailed as the timely application of a constitutional convention and the triumphant exercise of a constitutional remedy. The convention is familiarly known as the 'individual responsibility of Ministers'. The remedy, as *The Economist* expressed it, is that if Ministers 'fail to take early and effective action to counter potential miscarriages of justice or policy within their departments they must expect to step down from office'.

There is a good deal of constitutional folklore on this subject, to be true, but whether it adds up to a convention is very questionable.

THE SUPPOSED CONVENTION OF MINISTERIAL RESPONSIBILITY

'Each Minister', says Ivor Jennings, 'is responsible to Parliament for the conduct of his Department. The act of every Civil Servant is by convention regarded as the act of his Minister.'

This is as good a starting-point as any. The statement looks very clear. In fact there are three important obscurities. First, what is this 'Department' for which the Minister is said to be responsible? Next, what precise meaning is to be attached to the word 'responsible'? Thirdly, in what sense is the Minister rather than his civil servants regarded as 'responsible'?

Abridged from *Public Administration*, 34 (1956). © Royal Institute of Public Administration. Reprinted by permission of Basil Blackwell Limited.

1. *The Lowe Affair*, 1864

Lowe was accused of censoring the reports of HMIs contrary to Parliament's intentions, denied this, and was confronted with evidence produced by the HMIs themselves. Six days later he resigned, alleging that his honour had been impugned, and then explained that although the censorship was indeed continuing, contrary to his original statement to the Commons, he did not know this at the time; he had forbidden the practice, but could not know of its continuance because owing to his poor sight (he was nearly blind) he never read the reports but had them read to him. A Select Committee confirmed this story and later the House was told that Lowe's resignation 'was totally and entirely unnecessary'.

2. *The Captain Affair*, 1870–71

By the Order in Council of 1869 Childers, as First Lord, took responsibility for all that passed at the Admiralty. In 1870 the *Captain*, an ironclad of novel design, perished at sea with enormous loss of life. Despite the verdict of a court martial which acquitted the Chief Controller of blame, Childers, after an inquiry, published a minute laying responsibility on this Chief Controller, Sir Spencer Robinson. The case was vigorously debated in the Lords, but Sir Spencer was not reappointed to his office as Controller (the term of which had just expired) and was superseded in his other capacity of Third Lord.

3. *The Trafalgar Square Riots*, 1886

Childers took office as Home Secretary on the very day that serious riots took place in Trafalgar Square. Thereupon he secured the resignation of the Metropolitan Commissioner of Police (Henderson). *The Times* and other newspapers attacked him on the grounds that he was constitutionally responsible (as indeed he was) for the failure of police precaution, but Childers was easily able to show the Commons that he had only taken office at noon on the day of the riots and in the little time at his disposal had acted reasonably. He could not morally be held responsible, as the Opposition front bench itself confirmed.

4. *The MacDonell Affair*, 1904

Sir Anthony MacDonell became Permanent Under-Secretary to George Wyndham, the Irish Secretary, in 1902, on certain conditions made in an interchange of private letters and which gave him a wider latitude than is usual. Wyndham encouraged MacDonell to undertake negotiations with various Irish associations and personalities. A misunderstanding occurred. MacDonell wrote to Wyndham who was on holiday abroad to tell him that he was negotiating a scheme for devolution. Wyndham stuffed the letter unread into a book and forgot that he had ever received it. When he returned it was to to find *The Times* denouncing MacDonell's scheme. Wyndham immediately wrote to *The Times* repudiating the scheme. MacDonell, on seeing this, broke off his negotiations, and explained to his chief about the letter, an explanation which Wyndham accepted. The Cabinet, however, under pressure from their Ulster MPs censured MacDonell in an *aide-mémoire*, but acquitted him of acting disloyally. The Ulstermen, unappeased, demanded the resignation of Wyndham and the dismissal of MacDonell: the Liberal Opposition demanded the retention of both. Both sides pressed for the original terms of appointment. Wyndham, loyal to MacDonell and (in his own words) 'declining to retain office on [Irish] nationalist votes', resigned. He held himself responsible for not reading the fatal letter: and for not having given attention to the early negotiations as he ought to have done. The uproar in Parliament, and the pros and cons of MacDonell's conduct, however, continued to as late as 1906.

The case shows clearly, in the words of Sir David Maxwell Fyfe (now Lord Kilmuir) that: 'The Minister is not bound to approve an action of which he did not know or of which he disapproves' (*sic*). It also shows that, to avoid censure for the performance of an action, the Minister must be able to show clearly that he could not have prevented it and that the action would not recur. Since he had admitted to having received the letter he could not prove the first; since he refused to dismiss MacDonell he could not guarantee the second.

In conclusion, then, we can take the line that, when we speak of a Minister's individual responsibility we merely mean that, for every act or neglect on the part of civil servants, some Minister or other is charged to explain in the Houses of Parliament: and that only Ministers may do so.

Or, we can go further; we can add to the above that a Minister is answerable *for* the duties, albeit vicariously performed, with which he is charged. This will mean (on the basis of the precedents set out above) that arising out of or by reason of the expressed feeling of the House a Minister may be constrained (whether *in foro interno* or by pressure of his colleagues, or by the action of the Prime Minister) to tender his resignation on account of any act or neglect of his officers; it being understood that the Minister will not be held answerable for acts or neglects which he can prove he was clearly incapable of having known or prevented.

As we have seen, there is a strong tradition in favour of this interpretation. The question now arises as to whether such a convention is borne out by precedent. And for this it will be necessary to explore the history of ministerial resignations due, or apparently due, to the disapprobation of Parliament.

THE EFFECTIVENESS OF THE CONVENTION

Resignations 1855–1955

In what follows I have tried to particularize resignations which are not only 'forced' but, moreover, forced by overt criticism from the House of Commons. It is a somewhat subjective category of cases. To begin with, it excludes the very frequent cases where Ministers have voluntarily resigned— Mr Duff Cooper over the Munich affair, or (more recently) the resignations of Mr Bevan and Mr Wilson from the Attlee Government in 1951. It also excludes the considerably rarer cases where the whole Cabinet has chosen to go out rather than the individual under attack. Such was the case when Mr Chamberlain and his Cabinet resigned after the Narvik Vote in 1940. Mr Chamberlain was the Minister under attack.

Since, however, he was Premier, his resignation entailed, by convention, the resignation of the whole Cabinet. Thirdly, I have had to omit Ministers who quit or were 'dropped' from the Cabinet, sometimes upon the reconstruction of the Ministry, sometimes (apparently) in mid-career. Very often we do not know why they were dropped. In some cases—e.g. Salisbury's dismissal of Iddesleigh in 1886—we do know the reasons. But where such cases are, as it were, internal to the politics of the Cabinet, and not (overtly at any rate) initiated by the censure of the House of Commons, I have omitted them; for they palpably cannot be cited in support of the convention that Ministers are individually answerable *to the House* for the misconduct of their departments.

Bearing these qualifications in mind, it would seem that in the last century very few Ministers have resigned their offices in deference to the convention. The following list includes only senior Ministers. If not complete, it must be nearly so.

Lord John Russell	1855
Lord Ellenborough	1858
Robert Lowe	1864
Lord Westbury	1865
S. H. Walpole	1867
A. J. Mundella	1894
G. Wyndham	1905
Col. J. E. B. Seely	1914
A. Birrell	1916
A. Chamberlain	1917
N. Chamberlain	1917
Lord Rothermere	1918
E. S. Montagu	1922
Sir S. Hoare	1935
J. H. Thomas	1936
Viscount Swinton } Earl Winterton	1938
Sir Ben Smith	1946
H. Dalton	1947
Sir T. Dugdale	1954

The list does in fact contain two technically junior Ministers: viz., Lowe and Earl Winterton. Lowe was technically the junior to Lord Granville, the Lord President of the Council. Earl Winterton was, from 1937, Chancellor of the Duchy. In March 1938 he was given a seat in the Cabinet, and, with the style of 'Deputy Secretary of State for Air', became the junior colleague of Lord Swinton.

There are some important cases involving junior Ministers as well as senior. Among them may be mentioned Stansfeld (resigned 1864), Sir Robert Boothby (resigned 1941), and Belcher (resigned 1949).

These resignations fall into three not too well defined categories relating to (a) the man, (b) the personal act or policy, and (c) the vicarious act or policy—departmental mismanagement proper.

Collective Solidarity

The most effective of all the factors in thwarting the convention is, of course, the tendency on nearly every occasion for the Ministry to regard an attack on one of its members as an attack on itself and to throw itself as a buckler over the delinquent. It shielded Mr Shinwell from the attacks made on his handling of the fuel crisis in 1947; it shielded Mr Bevin and Mr Henderson (the unfortunate Secretary of State for Air) in the affair of the loss of the British Spitfires over Israel in January, 1949; it shielded Mr Strachey in the ground-nuts debate in the same year. In such cases, however restive, the majority party have but two alternatives—to pursue their vendetta and turn out their own Government (and, incidentally, themselves); or to drop the matter. They choose the latter.

> The ritual of each party is rehearsed
> Dislodging not one vote or prejudice;
> · The Ministers their Ministries retain
> And Ins as Ins, and Outs as Outs remain.

Low (1904) and Lowell (1908) both commented on the phenomenon. 'The party machine', wrote the first, 'always does intervene if the occasion is sufficiently serious to protect the departmental chief; so that the theoretical power residing in Parliament to bring about the dismissal of a Minister if he offends is not a very effectual check upon the conduct of any member of the Supreme Executive.' 'Joint responsibility', wrote the second, 'has in fact become greater, and the several responsibility less.' It is this fact that has induced Sir Ivor Jennings to regard individual responsibility as, in practice, an aberration from the common rule of collective responsibility; and to say of this: 'Ministers do get attacked. They are, however, defended by other Ministers, and the attack is really aimed not at the Ministers but at the Government. It may be convenient for a Prime Minister to promote a difficult Minister to a different office; but that is not the Opposition's intention; their principle anxiety is to cause the Government to lose votes at the next election.'

Nevertheless, ministerial resignations do take place; they are the exception, not the rule, but there are clearly occasions where the collective weight of the Ministry is *not* thrown into the scale. What special conditions have to operate for the convention of individual responsibility to end in resignation? They may be summarized as (i) where no party has an absolute majority in the House, and (ii) where the Minister's act has not so much offended the Opposition as alienated his own party, or a substantial element of it. The first needs no long explanation—it is enough to remark that the first five of our twenty precedents are governed by it. The second does, however, need explanation. It is still assumed that because parties tend to follow a rigid voting discipline on the floor of the House, they are therefore 'monolithic'. In fact, the tighter the floor discipline, imposed as it is by the need to remain in office and to win elections, the fiercer and more factious is the struggle for the party leadership. The parliamentary parties are full, always, of factions, of cabals, of Caves of Adullam.

Of the remaining fifteen instances, five are exceptional. Mundella and Dalton were placed in impossible personal situations. As to Austen Chamberlain, and Lord Rothermere also, there seems little doubt that had either wished to remain they could have done so. The first went, out of punctilio and contempt; the second, racked with insomnia and torn by private grief, out of indifference. The case of Neville Chamberlain, since he was not an MP or a party man, does not affect the hypothesis.

This leaves ten resignations to explain in terms of a 'backbench revolt.' Let us parade them in order.

1. *G. Wyndham* (1905). We have already shown that Wyndham could not remain in office if the extreme Unionists were to be placated. 'I should accept a decision of a majority of my own side and decline to retain office on Nationalist votes.'

2. *Colonel Seely* (1914). 'The idea that the Government had bargained with the officers for their return to duty was deeply repugnant not only to Liberals and Radicals but to a considerable number of others who were good House of Commons men and nothing could have saved the Government if Asquith had not been able to make it clear beyond doubt that he and the Cabinet had been prompt to correct the waverings of the military mind on the principles of the British constitution.'

3. *A. Birrell* (1916). Poor Birrell lost the support of all sides of the House except perhaps his faithful Irish Nationalists. As the *DNB* says, the condemnation was 'universal'.

4. *E. S. Montagu* (1922). 'Generally unpopular on personal grounds with the Conservative wing of the Coalition he had intensified this dislike by his attitude to General Dyer and it had long been clear that if he made a mistake he need expect no mercy from the majority in the House.'

5. *Sir S. Hoare* (1935). Lord Templewood's *Nine Troubled Years* is strangely uncommunicative as to the reasons which made the Cabinet change its mind from its initial support of his plan to the view that he must recant. He does, however, mention that the feeling in the Foreign Affairs Committee of the Conservative Members in the House of Commons had been violently antagonistic, and that the National Liberals also had condemned it. Petrie alleges that what decided the Cabinet was 'the fear that Austen [Chamberlain] would attack them . . . the Back Benches were flocking to him for a lead. . . . Mr. Baldwin was informed that Austen intended to lead the onslaught which would then be irresistible.' Tom Jones's account is substantially that of Lord Templewood: viz., that Austen Chamberlain had begun by trying to win over the back-benchers to the plan, but found the meeting so hostile that he could not maintain his view. But Jones also

adds what is confirmed from other sources, that Elliott, Duff Cooper, Oliver Stanley, and Ormsby-Gore, the younger Cabinet members, were against it.

6. *J. H. Thomas* (1936). There was no back-bench revolt in this case: but neither was there any faction to stand out for Thomas's retention. A Budget disclosure is, on all sides of the House, an irredeemable offence. Thomas was personally very popular with his Cabinet colleagues: but these never doubted that in the circumstances he had to go.

7 and 8. *Lord Swinton and Earl Winterton* (1938). These two resignations are associated. Since 1935 Lord Swinton had been Secretary of State for Air. In 1938 the Commons grew increasingly restive at our apparent lack of air defences, and the Prime Minister (Chamberlain) appointed Earl Winterton, who was Chancellor of the Duchy, to act as Deputy Secretary of State to Swinton, with a place in the Cabinet. In defending his estimates, on 12 May, Winterton completely failed to satisfy his critics, who were Conservatives as well as the Opposition. He resigned forthwith. Chamberlain decided that come what may, his Secretary of State for Air must be in the Commons, and asked Swinton to exchange his office for another. Swinton laid down his office, but declined to accept another—why, is not known. Earl Winterton retained the Duchy and his seat in the Cabinet till January 1939, when he became Paymaster-General.

Swinton's going was generally regretted in the House though it was felt that Earl Winterton had received no more than his deserts (a fact which, parenthetically, shows how freakish is the operation of the convention since the less worthy continued in office, and the more worthy suffered the penalty). There is evidence of back-bench pressure at work.

9. *Sir Ben Smith* (1946). It is not known whether there was a back-bench revolt of Labour Members against Sir Ben Smith: indeed the circumstances surrounding his dismissal are singularly obscure. His resignation was announced in *The Times* on 28 May 1946, together with a personal statement. In this he said he was 'very tired', and had wished to resign office on 5 April, but had stayed on in deference to the Prime Minister's wishes until the Lord President returned from his Washington mission. In the parliamentary debate on 31 May,

Mr Morrison denied that the resignation was due to policy differences, and equally that it was a 'dismissal'. Quoting Sir Ben's press statement, he gave the impression that the resignation was purely voluntary.

10. *Sir Thomas Dugdale* (1954). It is a fair inference from the distribution and the tenor of the speeches on the Conservative side that Sir Thomas had lost the confidence of at least the farmers' MPs. It was notable in the debate, also, that the Opposition were more tender towards him than were his own side. Evidently his back-benchers disliked the policy of his department as well as his administration, whereas many Labour MPs, applauded his policy and regretted his departure as a 'surrender of the 1947 Act'.

In the light of these examples, it seems then that a precondition of the fall of the Minister is either the fluidity of party lines or a back-bench revolt.

CONCLUSION

The convention implies a form of punishment for a delinquent Minister. That punishment is no longer an act of attainder, or an impeachment, but simply loss of office.

If each, or even very many charges of incompetence were habitually followed by the punishment, the remedy would be a very real one: its deterrent effect would be extremely great. In fact, that sequence is not only exceedingly rare, but arbitrary and unpredictable. Most charges never reach the stage of individualization at all: they are stifled under the blanket of party solidarity. Only when there is a minority Government, or in the infrequent cases where the Minister seriously alienates his own back-benchers, does the issue of the individual culpability of the Minister even arise. Even there it is subject to hazards: the punishment may be avoided if the Prime Minister, whether on his own or on the Minister's initiative, makes a timely re-shuffle. Even when some charges get through the now finely woven net, and are laid at the door of a Minister, much depends on his nicety, and much on the character of the Prime Minister. Brazen tenacity of office can still win a reprieve. And, in the last resort—though this happens infrequently—the resignation of the Minister may be made purely formal by reappointing to another post soon afterwards.

We may put the matter in this way: whether a Minister is forced to resign depends on three factors, on himself, his Prime Minister, and his party. On himself—as Austen Chamberlain resigned though possessing the confidence of his Prime Minister and his party, whereas Ayrton remained in office despite having neither. On the Prime Minister—as Salisbury stood between Matthews, his Home Secreary, and the party that clamoured for his dismissal. On the party—as witness the impotence of Palmerston to save Westbury, Balfour to save Wyndham, Asquith to save Birrell. For a resignation to occur all three factors have to be just so: the Minister compliant, the Prime Minister firm, the party clamorous. This conjuncture is rare, and is in fact fortuitous. Above all, it is indiscriminate—which Ministers escape and which do not is decided neither by the circumstances of the offence nor its gravity. A Wyndham and a Chamberlain go for a peccadillo, a Kitchener will remain despite major blunders.

A remedy ought to be certain. A punishment, to be deterrent, ought to be certain. But whether the Minister should resign is simply the (necessarily) haphazard consequence of a fortuitous concomitance of personal, party, and political temper.

Is there then a 'convention' of resignation at all?

A convention, in Dicey's sense, is a rule which is not enforced by the Courts. The important word is 'rule'. 'Rule' does not mean merely an observed uniformity in the past; the notion includes the expectation that the uniformity will continue in the future. It is not simply a description; it is a prescription. It has a compulsive force.

Now in its first sense, that the Minister alone *speaks* for his civil servants to the House and to his civil servants for the House, the convention of ministerial responsibility has both the proleptic and the compulsive features of a 'rule'. But in the sense in which we have been considering it, that the Minister *may be punished, through loss of office* for all the misdeeds and neglects of his civil servants which he cannot prove to have been outside all possibility of his cognizance and control, the proposition does not seem to be a rule at all.

What is the compulsive element in such a 'rule'? All it says
(on examination) is that if the Minister is yielding, his Prime
Minister unbending, and his party out for blood—no matter
how serious or trivial the reason—the Minister will find
himself without parliamentary support. This is a statement of
fact, not a code. What is more, as a statement of fact it comes
very close to being a truism: that a Minister entrusted by his
Prime Minister with certain duties must needs resign if he
loses the support of his majority. The only compulsive element
in the proposition is that if and when a Minister loses his
majority he ought to get out rather than be kicked out.

Moreover, even as a simple generalization, an observed
uniformity, the 'convention' is, surely, highly misleading? It
takes the wrong cases: it generalizes from the exceptions and
neglects the common run. There are four categories of
delinquent Ministers: the fortunate, the less fortunate, the
unfortunate, and the plain unlucky. After sinning, the first go
to other Ministries; the second to Another Place; the third just
go. Of the fourth there are but twenty examples in a century:
indeed, if one omits Neville Chamberlain (an anomaly) and
the 'personal' cases, viz., Mundella, Thomas, and Dalton,
there are but sixteen. Not for these sixteen the honourable
exchange of offices, or the silent and not dishonourable exit.
Their lot is public penance in the white sheet of a resignation
speech or letter. (Sir Ben Smith is the only exception: neither
shuffle nor white sheet for him, but highly uncommunicative
disappearance: Sir Winston put it as *spurlos versunken*, 'sunk
without trace'.) It is on some sixteen or at most nineteen
penitents and one anomaly that the generalization has been
based.

When Diagoras, the so-called atheist, was at Samothrace one of his
friends showed him several votive tablets put up by people who had
survived very dangerous storms. 'See,' he says, 'you who deny a
Providence, how many people have been saved by their prayers to
the Gods.' 'Yes,' rejoins Diagoras, 'I see those who were saved. Now
show me the tablets of those who were drowned.'

17

INDIVIDUAL RESPONSIBILITY: SOME POST-WAR EXAMPLES

GEOFFREY MARSHALL

If we look for instances of resignation by Ministers as the result of public or parliamentary criticism, there are since 1945 only about a dozen reasonably clear and one or two marginal cases. Of course, resignations are not always what they seem. Some that seem to be without fault[1] may be in anticipation of future dismissal (as perhaps was the resignation of Attlee's Minister of Food, Sir Ben Smith, in 1946). Some others that are on the face of it stout-hearted withdrawals as the alleged result of policy differences may in reality be polite expulsions or prudent subterfuges. It has been alleged, for example, that one of the Ministers who resigned from the first Wilson administration was required to retire on a false pretext as the result of information from the Security Service that he had put himself in serious danger of being blackmailed by Soviet bloc intelligence agents.[2] Of the overt cases, moreover, none involved a blameless Minister resigning as the result of departmental faults. Nor did any case between Sir Thomas Dugdale's Crichel Down resignation in 1954 and that of Lord Carrington over the Falkland Islands' occupation in 1982 involve an issue of political or departmental policy, though perhaps Mr James Callaghan's 1967 post-devaluation departure from the Exchequer in a sideways direction towards the Home Office might possibly be treated as such a case (as

Extracted from *Constitutional Conventions* (OUP, 1986). Reprinted by permission of Oxford University Press.

[1] There are, of course, a great many instances of genuine 'no fault' resignations as the result of policy disagreements, such as Mr Harold Wilson's resignation from the Attlee Cabinet or Mr George Brown's withdrawal from Mr Wilson's. These resignations are relevant to the unanimity aspect of the collective responsibility rule rather than to the rules of individual responsibility for failure in office.

[2] Chapman Pincher, *Inside Story* (1978), p. 17.

might Mr Emanuel Shinwell's translation from Fuel and Power to the War Office in 1947). All the rest involved questions of personal behaviour or alleged moral scandal. Dalton resigned in 1947 having prematurely handed out Budget information, and John Belcher in 1949 after the Lynskey Tribunal found him to have accepted small bribes for ministerial favours at the Board of Trade. They were followed in 1962 by Galbraith, blamed for consorting with the spy Vassall, and in 1963 by Profumo, blamed for consorting with Christine Keeler. Then in 1973 there was Lord Jellicoe who entertained call-girls under an assumed name and Lord Lambton who used his own. In 1974 a junior Minister in the Wilson Government, Lord Brayley, resigned after financial inquiries had been made into the affairs of a company with which he had previously been associated. Adverse publicity related to their private behaviour also accounted for the resignations of Mr Ian Harvey in 1958 and Mr Nicholas Fairbairn in 1982.

An arguable case for inclusion in the list is Mr Reginald Maudling who, having had dealings with the architect John Poulson, whose affairs were under investigation, resigned from the Home Office under the misapprehension that he was in charge of the police force. Home Secretaries seem particularly prone to mistakes of this kind. According to Lord Denning's report on the Profumo case, Mr Henry Brooke in 1963 did not know that he was head of the Security Service. For cases where a Minister does not know the nature and quality of his office we perhaps need a special category. We might call it 'diminished ministerial responsibility'.

As to vicarious liability for departmental subordinates, Ministers have never been keen on it. Both Mr Herbert Morrison and Sir David Maxwell Fyfe (as they then were), who spoke at some length about ministerial responsibility in the Crichel Down debate in 1954, were in agreement that resignation must entail some degree of personal culpability.

In considering what conclusions can be drawn about the convention of individual ministerial responsibility, it is useful to recall some of the well-known cases of non-resignations by Ministers when matters of one sort or another have gone wrong. The failure of the West African ground-nuts scheme in

Mr Attlee's post-war administration did not lead to the resignation of the nominally responsible Minister, Mr John Strachey. The Colonial Secretary Mr Lennox-Boyd did not resign when brutal treatment and killing of detainees at a prison camp at Hola in Kenya was debated in the House of Commons in 1959. In 1964 Mr Julian Amery did not resign when the Ministry of Aviation was found to have made large over-payments to Ferranti Ltd. for defence contract work. In 1971 the Vehicle and General Insurance Company collapsed and a Tribunal of Inquiry found that there had been negligence on the part of the Board of Trade in exercising its functions; but the President of the Board of Trade did not offer his resignation.

In the 1960s there were no ministerial resignations after the series of espionage scandals. Nor when large-scale miscalculations were made about the cost of the Concorde aircraft development programme. Nor again when sanctions against Rhodesia were evaded by the major oil companies with covert governmental acquiescence. In 1982 Mr William Whitelaw, as Home Secretary and police authority for the Metropolitan area, did not offer to resign when the arrangements for protecting the Queen and the security of Buckingham Palace were seen to be defective.

These cases divide into two categories. One category is that in which responsibility, i.e. culpability, is shared by a number of Ministers, and particular Ministers are protected by the assumption of collective responsibility. In relation to security failures, for example, Mr Harold Macmillan was apt to say in response to calls for resignations that the Government as a whole was responsible and that the electorate must judge it.

The other category is that in which the chain of command or accountability is extended either geographically or administratively, and mistakes have been made by someone of whom the Minister either has not heard or over whom he could not be expected to exert control or surveillance. Mr Lennox-Boyd could not be expected to have personal familiarity with the day-to-day operations of prison guards in Kenya, or Mr Whitelaw with the precise arrangements for patrolling the grounds of Buckingham Palace.

From these cases of non-resignation the current rules of

individual ministerial responsibility can be summarized. Sir Thomas Dugdale's resignation over the mishandling of his Department's policy towards the disposal of land revealed in the 1954 Crichel Down case, though it was accompanied by subordinate errors, was an assumption of personal responsibility by the Minister who had himself been involved in the particular misjudgement and who was held by his colleagues to have failed to organize his Department efficiently. He was not, as many alleged at the time, a Minister sacrificed in accordance with the hard doctrine that a ministerial head must roll for Civil Service error. No post-war case has involved such an assumption and it can be said with confidence that the convention of ministerial responsibility contains no requirement of any such vicarious accountability. Some Minister must of course answer in the House of Commons for Civil Service failings and must explain the reasons for their occurrence and the measures to be taken to prevent future failures. But the conclusions of Sir David Maxwell Fyfe in the Crichel Down debate in 1954 and the similar conclusions of the then Opposition spokesman Mr Herbert Morrison[3] may still be taken to state the present position. When action is taken of which a Minister disapproves and of which he has no prior knowledge, there is no obligation on his part to endorse it, to defend the errors of his officers, or to resign.

Lord Carrington's resignation in 1982, accepting personal responsibility for misjudgement of the danger from Argentina to the Falkland Islands (together with the resignations of the two junior Foreign Office Ministers Mr Richard Luce and Mr Humphrey Atkins), provides a further clear precedent for the existence of a rule requiring a Minister who is personally culpable of misjudgement or negligence to offer his resignation. In his survey of ministerial resignations some years ago, Professor S. E. Finer rightly observed that the supposed rule about ministerial resignations at the instance of the House of Commons was not based upon any sequence of precedents and therefore might be thought to be of doubtful authenticity. Perhaps Sir Thomas Dugdale and Lord

---

[3] See 530 HC Deb. 5s., col. 1278 et seq.

Carrington together do not constitute a sequence, or (since their downfall was not procured by the House of Commons) refute Professor Finer's thesis. None the less they are precedents and with a dash of principle may be treated as evidence of a convention whose existence is certainly not doubted in the House of Commons.

PERSONAL FAULT AND POLITICAL RESPONSIBILITY

Two recent ministerial departures, those of Mr Cecil Parkinson in 1983 and of Mr Leon Brittan in 1986, illustrate different facets of the convention of individual ministerial responsibility. Mr Parkinson resigned from his position as Secretary of State for Trade and Industry after publicity had been given to a long-standing affair with his secretary Miss Sarah Keays and after making a statement that he had decided not to marry Miss Keays, who had become pregnant by him, but to remain with his wife and family. Mr Parkinson's case raises at least one point of interest about the morality of political office. A number of ministerial resignations have been the result of personal faults or sexual irregularities. Earlier cases, however, such as those of John Profumo in 1963 and Lords Lambton and Jellicoe in 1973, were linked, whether plausibly or not, with possible security dangers and the need to avoid the possibility of blackmail arising from the activities of call-girls, the presence of Russian agents, and the dangers potentially arising from drug-consumption or sexual deviance. In the first of these cases there was the additional element of parliamentary affront arising from the Minister's misleading of the House of the Commons. These factors were set out at some length in the Denning Report of 1963 and in the reports of the Security Commission. Lord Denning was willing to specify at least some types of sexual misdemeanour that did not call for dismissal of public servants on security grounds. One of them was 'adultery committed clandestinely with a person not likely to resort to blackmail'. That description fits more or less exactly the situation of Mr Cecil Parkinson. Lord Denning's report, however, was not concerned with the political impact of clandestine relationships becoming publicly known. It might perhaps be inferred that Mr Parkinson's departure from office supports the conclusion that a constitutional convention or usage is emerging that Ministers are not to be allowed to treat deviation from conventional sexual morality as a private matter that need not impinge upon their continuance and effectiveness in public office.

On the other hand, the Prime Minister's first conclusion when Mr Parkinson's predicament became public knowledge was that no question of resignation arose. Several days later she apparently relinquished that belief. It is not entirely clear whether she changed her mind when a letter to *The Times* from Miss Keays gave further publicity to the affair. We do not know whether she then required Mr Parkinson to resign, or whether she failed to convey her own firm convictions to the Secretary of State and he insisted on leaving office despite being urged to remain.

So perhaps no new constitutional norm can be inferred from the episode. Past practice suggests that in the certain absence of any security danger the rules of comportment for Ministers of the Crown are a matter in which each Prime Minister and Cabinet are entitled to set their own standards, however conventional or peculiar. If it were to be decreed that all Cabinet Ministers were to wear red spotted handkerchieves on their heads at all times, no one's constitutional rights would be infringed, there being no entitlement to Cabinet membership. Ministerial chastity, we must conclude, is like the conventions of Cabinet secrecy and collective responsibility. It is a rule that can be suspended or breached except in circumstances when the Prime Minister, having considered the immediate and long-term political implications, feels it to be more honoured in the observance.

Mr Leon Brittan's resignation in January 1986 (also from the office of Secretary of State for Trade and Industry) adds to the small collection of post-war examples in which ministers have accepted responsibility for political or administrative misjudgement as distinct from private or personal misdemeanours. The only other clear instances are the resignations of Sir Thomas Dugdale as Minister of Agriculture after the Crichel Down affair in 1954 and Lord Carrington's resignation from the Foreign Secretaryship after the Falkland Islands invasion in 1982.

Mr Brittan's resignation was one of the consequences of a number of misunderstandings and failures of communication that occurred in the Government's handling of the Westland Helicopter Company affair in January 1986. The exact reason for Mr Brittan's resignation is not easy to state but perhaps it could be said to have arisen from an accumulation of misfortunes and misjudgements. The first was his failure to explain clearly to the House of Commons the facts about a confidential letter that had been received from British Aerospace PLC. For this he apologized to the House—a matter that might have been excused under the well-known doctrine of excusable ministerial error laid down by Mr Herbert Morrison in the Crichel Down debate in 1954. Mr Brittan's second misfortune was his authorization of the leaking by his press office of a critical letter written to the Secretary of State for Defence, Mr Michael Heseltine, by the Solicitor-General. Mr Brittan believed that his civil servants had obtained the agreement of the Prime Minister's office (and presumably the Prime Minister) to the disclosure made by his office. The Prime Minister's office and the Prime Minister claimed, however, that they had misunderstood what was being proposed, and the Prime Minister stated in the House that she had known nothing of Mr Brittan's role in the disclosure until she saw the results of an inquiry by the Cabinet Secretary sixteen days later. As with Mr Parkinson, we do not know exactly whether Mr Brittan insisted on resigning or was told to do so. But like Mr Parkinson he seems to have been abandoned when political and parliamentary criticism of his action persisted. His resignation adds a useful precedent to what previously looked a rather thin parade of examples that provide the evidence for the existence of a resigning convention for political error. The evidence now seems convincing.

18

MR BRITTAN'S CASE:
QUESTIONS AND ANSWERS

REPORT BY THE DEFENCE COMMITTEE

[*Note*: During the controversy over the affairs of the Westland Helicopter Company in 1985–6 a letter from the Solicitor-General to the Secretary of State for Defence was selectively disclosed to the Press by the Department of Trade and Industry. Both the Cabinet Secretary and the House of Commons Defence Committee held inquiries into responsibility for the disclosures.]

Did Mr Brittan have the Prime Minister's prior authority for the disclosure of the letter?

202. We asked Sir Robert Armstrong whether or not Mr Brittan had prior clearance from the Prime Minister, implicitly or explicitly, for the disclosure of the letter. Sir Robert said 'I naturally addressed that matter in the inquiry and I found absolutely no evidence whatever that he did, and I do not believe that he did.' However, during his inquiry Sir Robert Armstrong took evidence only from officials; the lack of evidence to which he refers indicates only that none of the officials concerned knew of such authorization. When he gave evidence a second time, however, Sir Robert confirmed his original view, saying that he had inquired further into the matter after finalizing his report; he had spoken to the Prime Minister and to Mr Brittan. He had also made other inquiries; he was unwilling to tell us what those inquiries were.

203. Mr Brittan told us that he 'did not get in touch with No. 10 on this between my communication of the view of the Solicitor-General [on Saturday 4 January] and acquiring knowledge that the letter had been written.' He also told us that he had no discussion with anyone in No. 10 before the disclosure. We asked Mr Brittan when he was first involved in

Extracted from the *Report from the Defence Committee of the House of Commons*, HC 519 (1985–6). Reprinted by permission of Her Majesty's Stationery Office.

discussions about releasing the information. He refused to tell us. We also asked Mr Brittan when he first spoke to anybody in No. 10 about the publication of the Solicitor-General's letter. Mr Brittan again refused to tell us.

Why did Mr Brittan not tell the Prime Minister he had authorized disclosure?

204. The Prime Minister has told the House that she did not know of Mr Brittan's role in the matter of the disclosure until Sir Robert Armstrong's inquiry had reported on 22 January. Sir Robert told us that he understood that the Prime Minister's words meant that 22 January was the first time that she knew that Mr Brittan had authorized the disclosure. We asked Mr Brittan whether or not he had any conversation with the Prime Minister, about the fact that he had authorized disclosure of part of the Solicitor-General's letter, before the Prime Minister received the report of the inquiry. He refused to tell us. When it was put to him that there was a period of time after the inquiry had been set up during which he knew what his role had been but chose not to inform the Prime Minister, he would not comment.

205. For the DTI officials at least, giving evidence to the Head of the Home Civil Service must have been a daunting and worrying experience. If, as the Prime Minister has repeatedly told the House, the DTI officials were confident that they had Mr Brittan's authority for the disclosure, and if, as Mr Brittan has confirmed, he gave them that authority, his silence during this time might be thought to have fallen short of the backing which a Minister normally gives his officials. We asked Mr Brittan whether he discussed with his private office or with other members of this staff the likely course or the actual course of the leak inquiry. Mr Brittan refused to tell us. (. . .)

The attendance of named officials

225. We sought oral evidence from three officials of the Department of Trade and Industry: Mr John Michell, Under-Secretary, Air Division; Mr John Mogg, Private Secretary to

the Secretary of State; and Miss Colette Bowe, Director of Information. The Permanent Secretary at the DTI, Sir Brian Hayes, informed the Clerk to the Committee that his Secretary of State, Mr Paul Channon

... is anxious that his Department should give all possible help to the Committee in its deliberations ... He does not however regard it as appropriate that officials you name should give evidence, and they will not therefore be accompanying me at the hearing.

226. We also sought oral evidence from Mr Bernard Ingham, Chief Press Secretary to the Prime Minister, and from Mr Charles Powell, a Private Secretary to the Prime Minister. The Secretary of the Cabinet informed the Clerk to the Committee that the No. 10 officials and the DTI officials:

gave a full account of their role in these matters to me in the course of my recent inquiry and co-operated fully in my investigation. The Prime Minister and the Secretary of State for Trade and Industry believe that your Committee will recognise and share their view that would be neither fair nor reasonable to expect these officials to submit to a second round of detailed questioning, of the sort that would be involved in giving evidence to your Committee.

With the Prime Minister's agreement, however, I am writing to you to say that, if the Committee believed that it would be helpful, I should be ready to accept an invitation to give evidence to the Committee. The basis of my evidence would of course be the comprehensive account of the matters in question which the Prime Minister gave the House of Commons on 23 and 27 January. I would hope, on the basis of my inquiry, to be able to deal as helpfully as possible with the Committee's questions, consistently with the normal conditions of confidence under which my inquiry was conducted.

227. Sir Robert Armstrong gave evidence to us on two occasions. He was not, however, prepared to name any individual official involved or to give any details of what they told him in his inquiry. As far as the actions of these officials was concerned, Sir Robert's evidence was, of course, hearsay. The evidence given by Sir Brian Hayes about the actions of the three officials in his Department was similarly hearsay; in addition, Sir Brian was under instructions from his Secretary of State not to answer on any matter covered by Sir Robert Armstrong's inquiry.

228. If a Select Committee has been given by the House the power to send for persons, papers, and records, its power to secure the attendance of an individual *named* civil servant is unqualified. (. . .)

230. Our request to have the five officials appear before us still stands. It became clear to us during our inquiry, however, that if we were to insist on these officials appearing before us, whether in public or in private, they would be under instructions from Ministers not to answer our questions. This could have placed them in an intensely embarrassing and unfair position, particularly if we had been forced to report to the House that their refusal to answer was impeding our inquiry.

231. The explicit authority of the House would have been necessary in order to override any ministerial instruction not to answer our questions. We considered asking for this authority, but wished to complete our inquiry, so far as was possible on the evidence before us, before reporting these circumstances to the House. This we now do.

232. *We do not accept the argument that when civil servants have had to give an account of their actions to an internal inquiry which has no formal status, those civil servants will be in double jeopardy if they subsequently have to give evidence on the same matters to a Select Committee.* The evidence which a witness gives to a Select Committee has the protection of absolute privilege; that is, the witness may not be proceeded against or disadvantaged on the grounds of the evidence which he has given.

233. Some witnesses may not see the formal protection afforded by privilege as a sufficient safeguard. As Sir Robert Armstrong said in evidence, in the case of the people concerned 'it is a question of their careers and reputations and lives'. In such circumstances, however, the responsibility lies with Ministers who require or expect officials to behave in an improper way, and with officials who comply.

Accountability to Parliament

234. At the heart of this problem lies the question of accountability to Parliament. The Treasury and Civil Service Committee have recently reported on the duties and

responsibilities of Ministers and civil servants, and during their inquiry had access to our evidence. In their Report the Treasury and Civil Service Committee did not question the prime loyalty of civil servants to the government of the day, but concluded that Ministers in their turn should hold themselves fully accountable to Parliament.

235. A Minister does not discharge his accountability to Parliament merely by acknowledging a general responsibility and, if the circumstances warrant it, by resigning. Accountability involves *accounting* in detail for actions as a Minister. The result of this may be that individual officials are shown to have acted improperly. More important, officials whose names would otherwise be unfairly associated with a discreditable episode may be shown to be blameless. The fact that Ministers have not made themselves fully accountable to Parliament in this matter has called into question the conduct of the civil servants involved.

236. This is particularly the case when the names of individuals are widely canvassed in the Press and elsewhere but a fiction of anonymity is maintained by Ministers and officials in the House in evidence to Select Committees.

237. *Ministers may express regret at the naming of individual officials in proceedings of the House. Yet when the conduct of individual officials is a matter of general comment and controversy, Ministers discharge their obligations to officials by satisfying the House that those officials have behaved properly. Officials who do their duty have a right to expect that support from their Ministers. If Ministers cannot demonstrate that officials have behaved properly, the question of disciplinary proceedings arises. (. . .)*

238. On the question of accountability as it relates to the matter into which we have been inquiring, the Treasury and Civil Service Committee concluded:

In the recent Westland case Sir Robert Armstrong was anxious to stress that neither he nor Ministers has named any of the officials involved but individual officials have certainly been named in the press. Whether or not an internal inquiry into various allegations had been made, we understand that no disciplinary action was taken in any case. We are not satisfied that a private internal inquiry which is not fully reported to Parliament constitutes accountability. The Defence Committee was told by Sir Robert it would have been unfair on the civil servants concerned to have been placed in double jeopardy by being examined on their behaviour by a Select Committee as well as being subject to an internal disciplinary inquiry. We do not find this a convincing argument. The officials concerned might well have welcomed the opportunity to explain their actions in public (which would not we stress have been in conflict with the confidential nature of advice to Ministers). It would have enabled Parliament to consider who was responsible for any msitakes and who ought to have been held accountable.

We endorse their view

19

THE DUTIES AND RESPONSIBILITIES OF CIVIL SERVANTS IN RELATION TO MINISTERS

Note by the Head of the Home Civil Service

ROBERT ARMSTRONG

1. During the last few months a number of my colleagues have suggested to me that it would be timely to restate the general duties and reponsibilities of civil servants in relation to Ministers. Recent events, and the public discussion to which they have given rise, have led me to conclude that the time has come when it would be right for me, as Head of the Home Civil Service, to respond to these suggestions. I am accordingly putting out the guidance in this note. It is issued after consultation with Permanent Secretaries in charge of departments, and with their agreement.

2. Civil servants are servants of the Crown. For all practical purposes the Crown in this context means and is represented by the Government of the day. There are special cases in which certain functions are conferred by law upon particular members or groups of members of the public service; but in general the executive powers of the Crown are exercised by and on the advice of Her Majesty's Ministers, who are in turn answerable to Parliament. The Civil Service as such has no constitutional personality or responsibility separate from the duly elected Government of the day. It is there to provide the Government of the day with advice on the formulation of the policies of the Government, to assist in carrying out the decisions of the Government, and to manage and deliver the

From *Ministers and Civil Servants*, February 1985. Reprinted by permission of Her Majesty's Stationery Office. (A slightly revised and expanded version—not differing in any essential detail—was published in *Hansard* on 3 December 1987.)

services for which the Government is responsible. Some civil servants are also involved, as a proper part of their duties, in the processes of presentation of Government policies and decisions.

3. The Civil Service serves the Government of the day as a whole, that is to say Her Majesty's Ministers collectively, and the Prime Minister is the Minister for the Civil Service. The duty of the individual civil servant is first and foremost to the Minister of the Crown who is in charge of the department in which he or she is serving. It is the Minister who is responsible, and answerable in Parliament, for the conduct of the department's affairs and the management of its business. It is the duty of civil servants to serve their Ministers with integrity and to the best of their ability.

4. The British Civil Service is a non-political and disciplined career service. Civil servants are required to serve the duly elected Government of the day, of whatever political complexion. It is of the first importance that civil servants should conduct themselves in such a way as to deserve and retain the confidence of Ministers, and as to be able to establish the same relationship with those whom they may be required to serve in some future Administration. That confidence is the indispensable foundation of a good relationship between Ministers and civil servants. The conduct of civil servants should at all times be such that Ministers and potential future Ministers can be sure that that confidence can be freely given, and that the Civil Service will at all times conscientiously fulfil its duties and obligations to, and impartially assist, advise, and carry out the policies of, the duly elected Government of the day.

5. The determination of policy is the responsibility of the Minister (within the convention of collective responsibility of the whole Government for the decisions and actions of every member of it). In the determination of policy the civil servant has no constitutional responsibility or role, distinct from that of the Minister. Subject to the conventions limiting the access of Ministers to papers of previous Administrations, it is the duty of the civil servant to make available to the Minister all the information and experience at his or her disposal which may have a bearing on the policy decisions to which the

Minister is committed or which he is preparing to make, and to give to the Minister honest and impartial advice, without fear or favour, and whether the advice accords with the Minister's view or not. Civil servants are in breach of their duty, and damage their integrity as servants of the Crown, if they deliberately withhold relevant information from their Minister, or if they give their Minister other advice than the best they believe they can give, or if they seek to obstruct or delay a decision simply because they do not agree with it. When, having been given all the relevant information and advice, the Minister has taken a decision, it is the duty of civil servants loyally to carry out that decision with precisely the same energy and good will, whether they agree with it or not.

6. Civil servants are under an obligation to keep the confidences to which they become privy in the course of their official duties; not only the maintenance of trust between Ministers and civil servants but also the efficiency of government depend on their doing so. There is and must be a general duty upon every civil servant, serving or retired, not to disclose, in breach of that obligation, any document or information or detail about the course of business, which has come his or her way in the course of duty as a civil servant. Whether such disclosure is done from political or personal motives, or for pecuniary gain, and quite apart from liability to prosecution under the Official Secrets Acts, the civil servant concerned forfeits the trust that is put in him or her as a servant of the Crown, and may well forfeit the right to continue in the Service. He or she also undermines the confidence that ought to subsist between Ministers and civil servants and thus damages colleagues and the Service as well as him or herself.

7. The previous paragraphs have set out the basic principles which govern civil servants' relations with Ministers. The rest of this note deals with particular aspects of conduct which derive from them, where it may be felt that more detailed guidance would be helpful.

8. A civil servant should not be required to do anything unlawful. In the very unlikely event of a civil servant being asked to do something which he or she believes would put him or her in clear breach of the law, the matter should be

reported to a superior officer or to the Principal Establishment Officer, who should if necessary seek the advice of the Legal Adviser to the department. If legal advice confirms that the action would be likely to be held to be unlawful, the matter should be reported in writing to the Permanent Head of the department.

9. Civil servants often find themselves in situations where they are required or expected to give information to a Parliamentary Select Committee, to the media, or to individuals. In doing so they should be guided by the general policy of the Government on evidence to Select Committees and on the disclosure of information, by any specifically departmental policies in relation to departmental information, and by the requirements of security and confidentiality. In this respect, however, as in other respects, the civil servant's first duty is to his or her Minister. Ultimately the responsibility lies with Ministers, and not with civil servants, to decide what information should be made available, and how and when it should be released, whether it is to Parliament, to Select Committees, to the media, or to individuals. It is not acceptable for a serving or former civil servant to seek to frustrate policies or decisions of Ministers by the disclosure outside the Government, in breach of confidence, of information to which he or she has had access as a civil servant.

10. It is Ministers and not civil servants who bear political responsibility. Civil servants should not decline to take, or abstain from taking, an action merely because to do so would conflict with their personal opinions on matters of political choice or judgement between alternative or competing objectives and benefits; they should consider the possibility of declining only if taking or abstaining from the action in question is felt to be directly contrary to deeply held personal conviction on a fundamental issue of conscience.

11. A civil servant who feels that to act or to abstain from acting in a particular way, or to acquiesce in a particular decision or course of action, would raise for him or her a fundamental issue of conscience, or is so profoundly opposed to a policy as to feel unable conscientiously to administer it in accordance with the standards described in this note, should consult a superior officer, or in the last resort the Permanent

Head of the department, who can and should if necessary consult the Head of the Home Civil Service.* If that does not enable the matter to be resolved on a basis which the civil servant concerned is able to accept, he or she must either carry out his or her instructions or resign from the public service—though even after resignation he or she will still be bound to keep the confidences to which he or she has become privy as a civil servant.

* The revised version of the memorandum states that a civil servant 'has a right in the last resort to have the matter referred to the Head of the Home Civil Service through the Permanent Head of the Department.'

20

CIVIL SERVANTS AND MINISTERS

REPORT BY THE TREASURY AND CIVIL SERVICE COMMITTEE

The Treasury and Civil Service Committee has agreed to the following Report:

INTRODUCTION

1.1. This Committee has been concerned about the relationship between Ministers and civil servants for some time. Long-term difficulties over manpower reductions, pay settlements, and promotion prospects have recently been exacerbated by the GCHQ Trade Unions affair and by the trial of a senior civil servant on charges under the Official Secrets Act. The Head of the Home Civil Service himself has admitted that there is a problem of morale in the Civil Service.

1.2. In response to some of these problems the Head of the Home Civil Service issued in February 1985 a Note of Guidance on the Duties and Responsibilities of Civil Servants in relation to Ministers. That note, now known after its author as the 'Armstrong Memorandum', gave rise to much comment both inside the Civil Service and more widely. This was the background to our decision to appoint a Sub-Committee to inquire into *Civil Servants and Ministers: Duties and Responsibilities*.

1.3. In the course of the Sub-Committee's inquiry, the so-called 'Westland Affair' dramatically exposed the difficult nature of relationships between Ministers, civil servants, and Parliament. In making this report to the House we have not examined deeply the detailed circumstances surrounding the Westland affair: other Select Committees are doing this. Our intention has been rather to deal with the longer term issues,

HC 92 (1985–6). Reprinted by permission of Her Majesty's Stationery Office.

since it is important that relationships between Ministers and their officials are such that the Civil Service is, and will remain, an effective and loyal instrument for any democratically elected government of any party acting within the limits of constitutional propriety.

1.4. Our Sub-Committee began the inquiry by writing to a large number of individuals and organizations requesting answers to a detailed questionnaire. We are grateful to all those who replied. In addition to receiving those written submissions, the Sub-Committee heard oral evidence from a wide range of witnesses. We are particularly grateful to Sir Robert Armstrong for his two appearances before the Sub-Committee. The oral evidence and the written appendices are important contributions to the current debate on civil servants and Ministers and we commend their study to all those who seek to reach conclusions in this area. In reaching our own conclusions, we have benefited from the enthusiastic and expert advice of Mr Andrew Likierman (London Business School) and Dr William Plowden (Royal Institute of Public Administration). (. . .)

3.14. It is to be hoped that such a statement would go some way towards the restoration of Civil Service morale, which Sir Robert said was a problem on which he was advising Ministers. The Council of Civil Service Unions told us that they would like to see 'positive decisions from Ministers to show that they are concerned about the morale in the Civil Service and they want to take positive steps to improve it'. Sir Douglas Wass hoped that 'perhaps Ministers could be reminded . . . of the need to recognise from time to time in public the loyalty and devotion that civil servants give to their ministerial chiefs'. We were also reminded by Lord Bancroft of his famous reference to: 'The ritual words of praise, forced out through clenched teeth in public [which] deceive no-one if they are accompanied by noisy and obvious cuffs around the ear in semi-private'. The Civil Service should not be a special case in this regard. Any enlightened employer will wish to balance criticism with praise. That is a basic principle of good management and in relation to the Civil Service it should also be a basic principle of good government.

Accountability

3.15. The issue of accountability is of crucial importance in considering the relationship between civil servants, Ministers, and Parliament. The traditional view, exemplified in the famous Crichel Down case, is that Ministers are responsible and accountable to Parliament for all that occurs within their departments. It followed from this that if a significant mistake were made by the department, the Minister should resign.

3.16. Recent events would seem to confirm what may well have been true for some thirty years, namely that Ministers are accountable for the Government's policies and their own actions or those carried out by civil servants on their specific instructions but not for actions by officials of which they are unaware. If this is correct, it raises most important questions which need to be carefully analysed and answered.

3.17. We start by reaffirming two basic propositions. First, that Ministers and not officials are responsible and accountable for policy, and secondly, that officials' advice to Ministers is and should remain confidential. These principles form the background to recent events and neither would appear to be in question. The difficulty arises not with regard to ministerial policy or official advice but with accountability for actions by civil servants. If Crichel Down is dead and Ministers are not accountable to Parliament for some actions of their officials, then who is? Not to put too fine a point on it, who ought to resign or to be penalized if mistakes are made? If it is not Ministers, it can only be officials. (. . .)

3.19. What are the options now? One would be to return to the Crichel Down doctrine. Alternatively a mechanism must be provided to make officials, in cases in which Ministers deny responsibility for their actions, accountable to Parliament. *We invite and recommend that the Government and other interested parties should produce for reconsideration specific proposals on how the crucial question of accountability should be dealt with in future.*

QUESTIONS OF PROCEDURE

4.1. How a civil servant should proceed when he is faced with a dilemma of the kind which raises matters of conscience or which challenges some basic assumptions about his duties or responsibilities is the practical question to which the Armstrong Memorandum was addressed. Sir Robert's answer is set out in the final paragraph to his note, where he says that such a civil servant 'should consult a superior officer, or in the last resort the Permanent head of the department, who can and should if necessary consult the Head of the Home Civil Service'. The Head of the Home Civil Service could then take the complaint up with the departmental Minister, or even with the Prime Minister. However, 'If that does not enable the matter to be resolved on a basis which the civil servant concerned is able to accept, he or she must either carry out his or her instructions or resign from the public service—though even after resignation he or she will be bound to keep the confidences to which he or she has become privy as a civil servant.' There is also the possibility of seeking a transfer to other work.

4.2. It is possible, but unproductive, to discuss the merits of these 'Armstrong procedures' in the abstract. It is better to look at specific examples, where they can be found. The best known case, although it precedes the February 1985 Memorandum (indeed, it led directly to the Memorandum) was that of Mr Ponting.

4.3. We cannot approve of Mr Ponting's behaviour. His dilemma concerned the way in which he was instructed to handle information concerning the sinking of the Argentine cruiser *General Belgrano*, and in particular what information should be conveyed to or withheld from Parliament. He took the view that he was being instructed to mislead Parliament, and so he sent anonymously some papers to Mr Tam Dalyell MP.

4.4. What should he have done? He could have resigned, but in that case he would not of course have been able to say why. The Armstrong Memorandum is 'only a restatement' of a doctrine going back at least fifty years, but we were told by Mr Ponting that 'there were no written guidelines at all in August 1984'. Nevertheless, even if Mr Ponting had used the established procedures which were available to him, it is by no means clear that he would have been able to resolve his predicament.

4.5. We were told by Mr Ponting that 'The Permanent Secretary was already aware of my views', and it seems that representations in writing had been made. As is now well known, the Permanent Secretary concerned did not choose to take up Mr Ponting's case.

4.6. Answering a parliamentary question on behalf of the Prime Minister in October 1985, the Leader of the House confirmed that no approaches had been made to Sir Robert Armstrong under the procedures since their restatement nearly six months previously. Since then, however, Sir Robert has himself had to conduct an inquiry which threw new light on the operation of his procedures. That inquiry was into the circumstances under which parts of the Solicitor-General's letter of 6 January to the then Secretary of State for Defence became public knowledge.

4.7. In the course of his inquiry, Sir Robert learnt that the official who was instructed to disclose the contents of the letter to the Press felt some disquiet and sought to consult the Permanent Secretary. The Permanent Secretary was not in London and due to the urgency of the situation he could not be consulted. Evidently, in such cases the 'Armstrong procedures' are of little use. Something more is needed.

A Code of Ethics

4.8. When there is no time to consult a Permanent Secretary, or when the Permanent Secreary refuses to take up a complaint, the aggrieved civil servant may need recourse to some written guidance on how best to proceed. The First Division Association has produced a draft of what it calls a code of ethics. In many respects, this code is an alternative statement to Sir Robert Armstrong's memorandum, covering much the same ground. Eventually, we understand, it is intended to incorporate a number of reforms which the FDA has under consideration but at this stage the code remains very much a general statement of principle.

4.9. It seems to us that if a code of ethics is to be of any real value, then it should attempt to cater for a wider and more specific range of circumstances than is provided for either in the FDA draft or in the Armstrong Memorandum. The FDA draft would have been no more use to the officials caught up in the Westland affair than was Sir Robert's note of guidance. But there are problems in producing a more detailed and comprehensive code. Mr Nevil Johnson doubted whether it would be possible to produce anything more than 'a statement of very loose principles which would not have any binding effect'. As the Liberal party's evidence reminded us, the code of ethics for government servants of the United States requires them to 'put loyalty to the highest moral principles and the country above loyalty to persons, party or government department'.

4.10. We were told in a paper submitted by the Cabinet Office that Sir Robert's note was no more than a restatement of principles. 'Nor was it intended that this statement of principles should prescribe in advance for every situation in which a civil servant might feel that his duty as a citizen conflicted with his duty to the Government which he serves.' We agree that it is probably impossible to make provision in a code of ethics for every conceivable dilemma which a civil servant could face in the course of his duties. However, we do believe that Sir Robert's note could be revised and expanded to cover a greater range of such situations, and in greater detail. It would then become, in effect, a code of ethics.

4.11. The work which the FDA has been doing should be put to good use by Sir Robert Armstrong in revising and expanding his note of guidance. *We recommend that the Head of the Home Civil Service should enter into discussions with the Civil Service Trade Unions with a view to producing an agreed text of a new note of guidance for civil servants.* Sir Robert's findings following his inquiry into the Westland leak confirmed that there will be some circumstances in which his procedures do not provide solutions. It makes sense now to seek to provide for such situations.

An Appeals Mechanism

4.12. Both Sir Robert's note of guidance and the FDA's code of ethics (as at present drafted) prescribe much the same procedure to be followed by civil servants who wish to resolve a dilemma of conscience: that is, reference up the hierarchy.

Sir Robert urges such people to 'consult a superior officer, or in the last resort the Permanent Head of the department, who can and should if necessary consult the Head of the Home Civil Service'. The FDA's code follows a similar route, except that the Permanent Head may, depending on the situation, approach either the Parliamentary Commissioner for Administration or the Chairman of the appropriate House of Commons Select Committee. It is the FDA's intention to amend their code so as to provide for access 'to an appropriately constituted independent body'. In their view, 'if conflicts arise between Ministers and civil servants the way of resolving them is through Parliament to whom Ministers are responsible'.

4.13. This view has the support of several of our witnesses, who felt that it was unfair to expect an aggrieved civil servant to take his complaint to superiors who might be the very people whose instructions had given rise to that grievance. Sir Douglas Wass described for us his proposal that there should be an 'Inspector General' for the Civil Service. This figure

would not be removable by Ministers and he would operate in some sense in a judicial capacity. His function would be to hear complaints by a civil servant who felt that the Minister was acting in an improper way . . . If he thought there was substance in it he would take the matter to the Minister . . . and he would invite the Minister . . . to correct the improper behaviour in some way. Thereafter if the Minister declined it might be necessary, as a final safety valve of course, for the Inspector General to have the right to report, perhaps in camera, to the relevant Select Committee.

4.14. We can see advantages in the creation of some new form of appeals procedure. The problem is whether this should be an internal or external mechanism. Mr Peter Kellner told us: 'the existence of some form of independent machinery, and the right of officials to use it, is likely to encourage Ministers and officials to observe the rules and to seek to resolve disputes with the minimum of fuss or disturbance to the progress of the government's legitimate business'. When we asked the head of the Home Civil Service for his opinion, he said that he found the idea of an external mechanism of Ombudsman 'a very difficult concept to work

with, because it seems to me it is going greatly to compli-
cate the relationship between civil servants and their Ministers'. (. . .)

Official secrets

6.6. Many of those who support the case for a Freedom of
Information Act place it in the context of the repeal of section
2 of the Official Secrets Act 1911. It would seem to be essential
to include in any Freedom of Information Act some definition
of what information should not be free, and such a redefinition
of 'secret' could well, in the opinion of the Committee, be a
substitute for the now largely discredited section 2. This is a
wider question than that which we have to address.

6.7. The Official Secrets Act has a very direct bearing on
relations between civil servants and Ministers. Under the Act,
Ministers are regarded as being self-authorizing. They can
authorize officials to release information and in so doing they
in effect grant to them immunity from any prosecution under
the Act. Very senior civil servants are also regarded as being
self-authorizing. Authority can be 'expressed' or it can be
'implied'; in practice this means that any disclosure which
suits a Minister's purposes will be treated as authorized.

6.8. A civil servant who discloses any official information
without the authority referred to above has 'leaked' and has
committed an offence under section 2 of the Official Secrets
Act. However, as Sir Robert Armstrong told our colleagues on
the Defence Committee, a disclosure which is authorized is
not a leak.

This places all but the most senior civil servants in a very
difficult position. Every day, in small, inconsequential ways,
civil servants are breaking the Official Secrets Act in the
course of carrying out their duties on behalf of Ministers.
Their disclosures can be regarded as 'authorized', but on
occasions officials have clearly gone outside such authority.

6.9. *We cannot regard as justified any leak by a civil servant which is
designed to frustrate the policies or actions of a Minister.* We have
already proposed ways of dealing with situations where a civil
servant might experience a dilemma of conscience, but we see
no workable or just alternative to the principle that in the

absence of a Freedom of Information Act it is for Ministers, and not officials, to decide when and how official information should be disclosed. When a Minister makes a wrong decision, he should pay the price.

6.10. Civil servants who leak should be dealt with severely, but this should normally be through internal disciplinary procedures, not through the courts. As one witness told us: 'Civil servants should be as capable of dismissal as other employees of good employers, under proper safeguards against injustice to them. But the criminal law should be reserved for matters which injure the state, not those which merely—even if justifiably—upset other civil servants or Ministers.' *Civil servants who leak information should face the sack or internal discipline.*

6.11. Where 'matters which injure the state' are concerned, there will clearly remain a need for legislation which will continue to provide for recourse to the courts. Again, we have not inquired into this in sufficient depth to pronounce on the precise form such legislation should take. It is for the Government, not this Committee, to propose legislation. However, *in our view section 2 of the Official Secrets Act is now unenforceable.*

21

SECRECY, DISCLOSURE, AND THE PUBLIC INTEREST

YVONNE CRIPPS

In the case of *Commonwealth of Australia* v. *John Fairfax & Sons Ltd.*,[1] Mason J described the action for breach of confidence in terms of an equitable principle.[2] He remarked that

the equitable principle has been fashioned to protect the personal, private and proprietary interests of the citizen, not to protect the very different interests of the executive government. It acts, or is supposed to act, not according to standards of private interest but in the public interest. This is not to say that Equity will not protect information in the hands of the government, but it is to say that when Equity protects government information it will look at the matter through different spectacles . . . It is unacceptable, in our democratic society, that there should be a restraint on the publication of information relating to government when the only vice of that information is that it enables the public to discuss, review and criticise government action. Accordingly, the court will determine the government's claim to confidentiality by reference to the public interest.[3]

This is compelling reasoning in the context of the action for

From *Public Law* (1983), pp. 619–23, 630–3. Reprinted by permission of Stevens & Sons Limited.

[1] (1980) 32 ALR 485. The disclosures in the *Fairfax* case involved the publication of confidential information which concerned, *inter alia*, the role of the Australian Government with regard to the crisis in East Timor.

[2] Cf., however, Jones, 'Restitution of Benefits Obtained in Breach of Another's Confidence' (1970) 86 *LQR* 463, and *Breach of Confidence*, Law Com. No. 110 (Cmnd. 8388, 1981), p. 10.

[3] *Commonwealth of Australia* v. *John Fairfax & Sons Ltd.* (1980) 32 ALR 485, 492–3. Note that the Public Records Acts of 1958 and 1967 establish that public records will normally be released after they have been in existence for 30 years: s. 5 (1) (*a*) of the Public Records Act 1958; see also s. 10 of and Sched. 1 to the Public Records Act 1958 for a definition of public records. Under s. 5 (1) (*b*) of the Act of 1958 (as amended by s. 1 of the Act of 1967), the Lord Chancellor may specify a period of more or less than 30 years with regard to any particular class of public records.

breach of confidence.⁴ Is it equally compelling in relation to information governed by the Official Secrets Acts? Should Parliament pass an amendment which would exclude public interest disclosures from the ambit of official secrets legislation?

Numerous criticisms have been made of the scope of the Official Secrets Acts and of excessive secrecy in central and local government.⁵ For instance, the members of JUSTICE have commented that under the Official Secrets Acts, 'the disclosure or improper use of the most harmless document can lead to a prosecution . . . this does not make for good government since it can lead to protection of inefficiency and malpractice, stifle the needful exposure of public scandals, and prevent the remedying of individual injustices'.⁶ JUSTICE recommended that 'it should be a valid defence in any prosecution under the Official Secrets Act to show that the national interest or legitimate private interests confided to the State were not likely to be harmed and that the information was passed and received in good faith and *in the public interest*'.⁷

In response to these proposals,⁸ Mr Jasper More, MP, introduced the Freedom of Publication Bill 1968 as a Private Member's Bill. Clause 3 (1) of the Bill contained the following words: 'A person shall not be guilty of an offence under section

---

⁴ See *Breach of Confidence*, Law Com. No. 110, op. cit. at pp. 138–41.

⁵ See, e.g. Williams, *Not in the Public Interest* (1965); *Report of the Committee on the Civil Service* (Cmnd. 3638, 1968), p. 92; Williams, 'The Control of Local Authorities', in Andrews (ed.), *Welsh Studies in Public Law* (1970), at pp. 117 and 121–3; *Second Report of the Royal Commission on Environmental Pollution*, 'Three Issues in Industrial Pollution' (Cmnd. 4894, 1972), paras. 3–10; *Report of the Departmental Committee on Section 2 of the Official Secrets Act 1911* (Cmnd. 5104, 1972); R. Dworkin, 'Open Government or Closed?', *New Society*, 24 June 1976, p. 679; JUSTICE, *Freedom of Information* (1978); Cornford, *Official Information* (1979), 31 *Aslib Proceedings* 427; 'Health Warnings Kept Secret by Whitehall', *The Sunday Times*, 2 Dec. 1979, p. 5; 'Council Planners Say Government Department is Hiding Behind Secrets Act Over Nerve Gas Move', *The Times*, 12 May 1980, p. 4; 'Minister is Challenged Over Secrecy on Fast-Breeder Reactor', *The Times*, 7 July 1980, p. 4, and Delbridge and Smith (edd.), *Consuming Secrets: How Official Secrecy Affects Everyday Life in Britain* (1982).

⁶ JUSTICE, *The Law and the Press* (1965), 21.

⁷ Ibid. at p. 23 (emphasis added). See also Williams, 'Official Secrecy in England', loc. cit. at p. 35 and James Callaghan's submission to the Franks Committee, discussed on p. 38 of the Franks Report.

⁸ See HC Deb., Vol. 758, col. 951, 12 Feb. 1968; HC Deb., Vol. 764, cols. 819 et seq., 10 May 1968; HC Deb., Vol. 776, cols. 1709 et seq., 31 Jan. 1969; and HL Deb., Vol. 274, cols. 1371 et seq., 25 May 1966.

2 (2) of the Official Secrets Act 1911 as amended by section 10 of the Official Secrets Act 1920 . . . if he establishes that the act of which he is accused was not prejudicial to the public interest.' Although, in one sense, this was narrower than the JUSTICE proposal, which did not appear to be confined to section 2 (2) of the Act of 1911,[9] the Bill was received with a degree of caution which has been characteristic of governmental attempts to reform the law relating to official secrets.[10]

In 1969, the then Labour Government commented:

It has sometimes been suggested that the scope of [the Official Secrets Act] ought to be limited, so that it would not be an offence to disclose official information without authority unless national security or some other major public interest were directly involved. There would, however, be the greatest difficulty in defining satisfactorily what categories of information should qualify for this special protection and what should not, because the range of information which may need this protection is so varied.[11]

These remarks suggest that the Government was of the opinion that the courts are not well suited to the task of determining whether certain disclosures will harm the public interest. Indeed, the members of the Franks Committee also envisaged a system of official secrecy in which the courts would play a restricted role.[12] They proposed a series of classifications which they wished to see linked with the criminal law. Under the Franks proposals, information which, if disclosed, would cause serious or extremely

---

[9] In another sense, the Bill places a lesser burden on the accused than was proposed by JUSTICE. The Bill, if implemented, would have required the accused to establish that his actions were *not prejudicial to the public interest*. The JUSTICE proposal would have relieved an accused of liability only if he could demonstrate that his actions were *in the public interest*.

[10] See, e.g. the protection of Official Information Bill 1979. The Bill received its second reading in the House of Lords on 5 Nov. 1979, but was withdrawn by the Government on 20 Nov. 1979, as a result of considerable criticism, much of which related to the fact that, if it were to be passed into law, such an Act would prohibit disclosures of the kind which led to the revelations about Anthony Blunt's role in passing official secrets to the Soviet Union.

[11] *Information and the Public Interest* (Cmnd. 4089, 1969), paras. 32–3.

[12] See also the then Labour Government's response to the Franks Report, *Reform of Section 2 of the Official Secrets Act 1911* (Cmnd. 7285, 1978). Cf., however, cl. 3 (3) of the Freedom of Publication Protection Bill 1968.

serious injury to the interests of the nation would be marked 'Secret' or 'Top Secret' and its disclosure would give rise to criminal sanctions.[13] Less injurious disclosures would be dealt with, where appropriate, by means of work-place disciplinary measures rather than the criminal law.[14] The continuing accuracy of a classification would be verified at the time of the disclosure by a certificate from the responsible Minister. The members of the Committee also proposed that 'The Minister would take personal responsibility for the judgment that this was a disclosure which would cause serious injury to the interests of the nation, and would be answerable in Parliament for his decision'.[15] They noted that a number of witnesses had put forward proposals which would have involved the courts in deciding whether a disclosure had caused injury to the nation. The members of the Committee remarked that in several cases the proposals had been made on the basis that it should be a defence to a charge under section 2 that the disclosure in question was not likely to harm the national interest and was made in good faith and in the public interest. In response to these proposals, the Committee concluded: 'We considered whether such a responsibility could appropriately be placed upon the courts, but decided that it could not.'[16]

The reasons which the Committee presented in support of that conclusion were not convincing. The Committee's first objection was that juries would find it difficult to deal with contentious political issues of the kind which could arise in prosecutions under the Official Secrets Acts.[17] Yet that argument concerns the inadequacy of juries rather than

---

[13] See pp. 55 ff. of the Franks Report.

[14] For example, the Committee expressed the view that disclosures regarding the budget or the bank rate did not warrant the sanction of the criminal law. Information about such matters would not be classified as 'Secret' or 'Top Secret'. See pp. 52, 57, 63, and 64 of the Franks Report. See also *Budget Disclosure Inquiry, Report of the Tribunal Appointed under the Tribunals of Inquiry (Evidence) Act 1921* (Cmd. 5184, 1936) and *Report of the Tribunal Appointed to Inquire Into Allegations of Improper Disclosure of Information Relating to the Raising of the Bank Rate* (Cmnd. 350, 1958).

[15] See p. 61 of the Franks Report.

[16] Ibid. at p. 55.

[17] Ibid. In the separate context of the public interest defence to the action for breach of confidence, the members of the Law Commission, in their report on breach of confidence, also came to the conclusion that juries were not the best assessors of the public interest. See *Breach of Confidence*, Law Com. No. 110, op. cit. at p. 162.

judges. In addition, the members of the Committee referred to what they described as certain 'relatively recent' decisions of the House of Lords which indicated that the House was reluctant to consider arguments concerning the national interest as regards matters of defence and foreign relations.[18] But the Committee did not attempt to say why such reluctance was appropriate or desirable.[19]

The members of the Franks Committee also noted that the assessment of the damage which could be caused by a particular disclosure would 'depend very much' on the surrounding circumstances.[20] The Committee suggested that the timing of a disclosure could be an extremely crucial factor in this context. But instead of regarding this as an argument in favour of allowing the courts to examine whether particular disclosures are contrary to the public interest, or indeed in the public interest, the Committee employed the argument to justify its conclusion that the sole responsibility for the classification and assessment of official information should lie with the Government. It stated: 'Any system which placed this responsibility elsewhere would detract from the responsibility of the Government to protect the security of the nation and the safety of the people. It would remove the element of constitutional accountability.'[21] It has, however, been suggested that the Franks Committee's reliance on ministerial responsibility was misplaced. Even if Members of Parliament request the Minister to explain his actions in the Commons, there is no reason to suppose that information which can be presented in an open parliamentary forum should not be presented to the courts.[22]

In view of the unwillingness of successive governments to undertake sweeping reform of official secrets legislation,[23] it would be desirable if cases like *Attorney-General* v. *Jonathan Cape*[24] and *Commonwealth of Australia* v. *John Fairfax & Sons Ltd.*[25] were to lead the legislature to an appreciation of the fact

---

[18] Two relevant decisions of the House of Lords which were 'relatively recent' at the time of the publication of the Franks Report are *Conway* v. *Rimmer* [1968] AC 910 and *Norwich Pharmacal Co.* v. *Commissioner for Customs and Excise* [1974] AC 133.

[19] See Jacob, 'Some Reflections on Governmental Secrecy', (1974) *PL* 25, 42.

[20] Ibid. at p. 54.

[21] Ibid. at p. 54.

[22] Ibid. at p. 42.

[23] e.g. see n. 10, above.

[24] [1976] QB 752.

[25] (1980) 32 ALR 485.

that it is time to reconsider the possibility of a modest amendment to the Official Secrets Act 1911.[26] Such an amendment would provide that an accused would have a defence to a prosecution under the Official Secrets Acts if he could establish that he acted in good faith and that the conduct of which he is accused was in the public interest.[27] A limited reform of that nature would be more likely to find favour with the Government than a proposal based on the desirability of freedom of information and informed public debate.[28] A proposal based directly on the latter considerations would relieve an accused of liability if he demonstrated that his actions were not prejudicial to the public interest, rather that they were *in* the public interest.[29]

Some of the statutory provisions which prohibit disclosure without referring to a specific defence of disclosure in the public interest might, however, be construed in a manner which enables those who disclose information to escape liability if they can satisfy the court that disclosure was in the public interest. For example, section 45 of the Telegraph Act 1863 and section 11 of the Post Office (Protection) Act 1884 describe the penalties which may be incurred by a Post Office employee who 'improperly divulges' the content of a message. Section 20 of the Telegraph Act 1868 prohibits the disclosure or interception of messages by a Post Office employee 'contrary to his duty'. If an employee's disclosure is made in the public interest, can it be argued that he has not divulged information 'improperly' or 'contrary to his duty'? There is certainly no legal duty to disclose information which the public has an interest in receiving.[30] The problem in this context is that of ascertaining the nature and extent of the

---

[26] See above, with regard to the original JUSTICE recommendation.

[27] This reform should be accompanied by a reduction of the basic 30-year period before which so-called 'public' records are not normally made publicly available. See s. 5 of the Public Records Act 1958 and n. 3, above.

[28] See above. The *Jonathan Cape* and *Fairfax* cases, which concerned civil actions for breach of confidence, went even further towards facilitating disclosure. They placed the onus of proof on plaintiffs by requiring them to satisfy the courts that there is a public interest in upholding claims concerning the undesirability of the disclosure of the information in question.

[29] See e.g. the Freedom of Publication Protection Bill, discussed above.

[30] The same comment applies to s. 65 of the Post Office Act 1969, which exempts employees from an obligation of secrecy 'in such cases as may be required by law'.

employee's duty to refrain from disclosing information. A disclosure that is made in the public interest ought not to be classified as an 'improper' disclosure.

Paragraph 1 of Schedule 5 to the Post Office Act 1969 states that a person charged with an offence under section 45 of the Telegraph Act 1863, section 11 of the Post Office (Protection) Act 1884, or section 20 of the Telegraph Act 1868 can defend himself by proving that his actions were carried out 'in obedience to a warrant under the hand of a Secretary of State'. The existence of an express statutory defence to those sections should not, however, be interpreted in such a way as to preclude a court from taking other defences into account.

Statutes that contain penal provisions prohibiting the disclosure of information which is entrusted to various individuals and authorities[31] should expressly provide for a defence of disclosure in the public interest. It would not be desirable to propose a standard statutory formula for such a defence. Defences of disclosure in the public interest in the context of infringements of statutory obligations to refrain from disclosure should be tailored to meet the requirements of the statutory provisions that prohibit disclosure. The various statutory formulae already adopted for the purpose of providing a public interest defence illustrate the need for specificity.[32] Such provisions should, where appropriate, be included in a new legislation and added to existing legislation.[33]

CONCLUSION

In a working paper on the subject of breach of confidence, the Law Commission stated that it is 'a cardinal principle of any democratic society that restrictions should not be imposed on

---

[31] See *Breach of Confidence*, Law Com. No. 110, op. cit. at pp. 96 ff and 123 for a discussion of whether obligations of confidence attach to such information in the hands of its recipients.

[32] See e.g. s. 3 (1) of the Finance Act 1967; s. 19 (4) (a) of the Banking Act 1979; s. 8 (3) of the Parliamentary Commissioner Act 1967.

[33] In this way it should be possible to eliminate existing ambiguities in statutes which prohibit disclosures that are 'improper', 'corrupt', or 'contrary to (an individual's) duty'. See e.g. s. 45 of the Telegraph Act 1863; s. 11 of the Post Office (Protection) Act 1884; s. 20 of the Telegraph Act 1868; s. 1 of the Public Bodies Corrupt Practices Act 1889; and s. 1 of the Prevention of Corruption Act 1906.

the truth except to the extent that they are necessary to protect individuals or society as a whole from a real likelihood of damage'.[34]

Such sentiments are also relevant outside the sphere of the action for breach of confidence, with its associated remedy of an injunction to prevent disclosure. Injunctions of that kind involve prior restraint, a concept which, in general, civil libertarians tend to decry. Yet prior restraint can exist in other guises. In a formal sense, it may be possible to obtain an injunction to prevent a breach of section 2 of the Official Secrets Act 1911. In the *Fairfax* case, the High Court of Australia refused to grant an injunction to restrain a breach of section 79 of the Crimes Act 1914 (Cth.).[35] Mason J quoted the words of Lord Wilberforce in *Gouriet* v. *Union of Post Office Workers* to the effect that the practice of granting an injunction to prevent a breach of the criminal law 'is confined, in practice, to cases where an offence is frequently repeated in disregard of a, usually, inadequate penalty . . . or to cases of emergency'.[36] He concluded that section 79 created a criminal offence which carried with it substantial penalties but no right to injunctive relief.[37] He did, however, acknowledge that 'It may be that in some circumstances a statutory provision which prohibits and penalises the disclosure of confidential government information or official secrets will be enforceable by injunction'.[38] None the less, Mason J's views on the limited nature of the Attorney-General's prospects of obtaining an injunction for the purpose of restraining a breach of the criminal law appear to be somewhat restrictive. De'Smith, for example, is more confident about the Attorney-General's chances of success in this context, although he does recognize

---

[34] *Breach of Confidence*, Law Com. No. 58 (1974), at p. 50. See also the final report of the Law Commission, *Breach of Confidence*, Law Com. No. 110, op. cit. at pp. 3, 91, 92, and 140.

[35] s. 79 is the Australian equivalent of s. 2 of the Official Secrets Act 1911.

[36] *Gouriet* v. *Union of Post Office Workers* [1978] AC 435, 481. See Williams, 'Preventive Justice and the Courts', (1977) *Crim.LR* 703 and 'The Prerogative and Preventive Justice' (1977) *CLJ* 201. See, more generally, *R.* v. *Inland Revenue Commissioners, ex p. National Federation of Self-Employed and Small Businesses Ltd.* [1982] AC 617 and Peiris, 'The Doctrine of *Locus Standi* in Commonwealth Administrative Law', (1983) PL 52.

[37] *Commonwealth of Australia* v. *John Fairfax & Sons Ltd.* (1980) 32 ALR 485, 491.

[38] Ibid.

that the competence of the Attorney-General to obtain injunctions in respect of unlawful conduct is not unlimited and that some statutes specifically empower the Attorney-General or the Crown to institute civil proceedings in order to restrain individuals from violating the provisions of the statutes in question.[39]

Even if the courts will not grant injunctions for the purpose of enforcing the prohibitions on disclosure that are contained in the Official Secrets Act, *informal* prior restraint almost certainly exists in terms of the fears of Crown servants who know that they cannot rely on a public interest in disclosure in order to defend themselves against the disciplinary action which is likely to follow unauthorized disclosures of official information. For instance, Daniel Ellsberg, in discussing the *Pentagon Papers*,[40] remarked that the main obstacle he had had to overcome before revealing the contents of the Papers 'was the psychological one of even imagining that you might reveal such information, if you have worked in the executive branch for more than a decade as I have . . . In other words, the whole way of life in the executive branch is such that violating agency secrecy is not an option that you are constantly weighing in your mind, but rather an unthinkable move.'[41]

In this country, public-spirited employees cannot point to a constitutional guarantee of free speech,[42] or to freedom of information legislation.[43] They do, however, deserve the protection of public interest defences of the kind described in this article. Sporadic disclosures of information by public sector employees will never represent an adequate substitute for legislation providing for a right of access to official information. In the absence of such legislation,

---

[39] See Evans (ed.), *de Smith's Judicial Review of Administrative Action* (4th edn., 1980), at pp. 453–4. In *Attorney-General* v. *Jonathan Cape Ltd.* [1976] QB 752, the Attorney-General did not seek an injunction in respect of a breach of the Official Secrets Acts.

[40] Ellsberg's views were recorded in an interview conducted in Sept. 1981 and published in Peters and Branch, *Blowing the Whistle* (1972), p. 246.

[41] Ibid. at p. 250.

[42] The First Amendment to the United States Constitution guarantees that 'Congress shall make no law . . . abridging the freedom of speech, or of the press, or the right of the people peaceably to assemble, and to petition the Government for a redress of grievances'.

[43] Cf. the Public Information Act 1967 (5 USC, s. 552) and see Boyle, 'Freedom of Expression as a Public Interest in English Law', [1982] *Public Law* 574.

however, they provide one of the few sources from which information about the activities of government can be acquired. Even if a Freedom of Information Act were to be passed,[44] disclosures of information by employees would still serve an important purpose. A statute which simply enables members of the public to have access to information does not serve the function of drawing the community's attention to particular governmental activities. The utilization of such a statute, in terms of a request for information, normally presupposes that the individual who makes the request knows of the existence of a specific set of documents or course of correspondence. Accordingly, employees will often be in the best position to raise the initial alert about the activities of their public sector employers. They should not be left without defences to the prejudicial actions of those whom, in the public interest, they seek to expose.

[44] A Freedom of Information Bill, introduced as a Private Member's Bill by Frank Hooley, MP, failed to receive a second reading in the Commons. See HC Deb., Vol. 998, cols. 514–82, 6 Feb. 1981, and 'Information Bill Looks Doomed to Failure', The Times, 7 Feb. 1981, pp. 1 and 2, and 'Progress of Bill Halted', The Times, 7 Feb. 1981, p. 3. Note that President Reagan intends to reduce the scope of the United States Freedom of Information Act. See 'Revolting Women Rattle the CIA', The Sunday Times, 3 Jan. 1981, p. 4. See also 'New CIA Code of Conduct', The Times, 5 Feb. 1982, p. 9, and 'President Moves to Plug the leaks', The Times, 14 Jan. 1983, p. 6.

LIST OF AUTHORS

SIR ROBERT ARMSTRONG, Head of the Civil Service 1983–7 and Secretary to the Cabinet 1979–87.

A. H. BIRCH, Professor of Political Science at the University of Victoria, British Columbia.

D. E. BUTLER, Fellow of Nuffield College, Oxford.

SIR NORMAN CHESTER (1907–86), Warden of Nuffield College, Oxford, 1954–78.

YVONNE CRIPPS, Director of Studies in Law, Emmanuel College, Cambridge.

A. V. DICEY (1835–1922), Vinerian Professor of English Law and author of *Introduction to the Study of the Law of the Constitution* (1st edition, 1885).

J. LL. J. EDWARDS, Professor of Law and Director, Centre of Criminology, University of Toronto.

DAVID ELLIS, Barrister at Law.

S. E. FINER, Gladstone Professor of Government and Public Administration, Oxford University, 1974–82, now Professor-Emeritus.

PETER HENNESSY, Political Researcher and Consultant Editor of the Institute of Contemporary British History.

LORD HUNT OF TANWORTH, Secretary of the Cabinet, 1973–9.

SIDNEY LOW, Historian and author of *The Governance of England* (1904).

GEOFFREY MARSHALL, Fellow of The Queen's College, Oxford.

LORD MORLEY, (1838–1923), Liberal Statesman, essayist and biographer.

I. F. NICOLSON, Author of *The Mystery of Crichel Down* (OUP 1986).

PHILIP NORTON, Professor of Politics, University of Hull.

ARTHUR SILKIN, Ex-civil servant.

LORD WILSON OF RIEVAULX, Prime Minister, 1964–70 and 1974–6.

SELECT BIBLIOGRAPHY

Ministerial Responsibility: Historical Development

ANSON, Sir W., *The Law and Custom of the Constitution* (4th edn., ed. A. B. Keith), vol. ii, pt. 1, 'The Crown'.

BIRCH, A. H., *Representative and Responsible Government* (1964), chaps. 2–3.

CHESTER, Sir N., *The English Administrative System 1780–1870* (1981).

HANHAM, H. J., *The Nineteenth-Century Constitution: Documents and Commentary* (1969).

LOWELL, A. L., *The Government of England* (rev. edn. 1919), vol. i, chaps. 2–3.

COLLECTIVE RESPONSIBILITY

ALDERMAN, R. K., and CROSS, J. A., *The Tactics of Resignation* (1967).

BRAZIER, R. *Constitutional Practice* (1988) Chap. 6.

CHESTER, D. N., 'Parliamentary Questions', in *The Commons Today*, ed. M. Ryle and S. A. Walkland (1981).

ELLIS, D. L., 'Collective Ministerial Responsibility and Solidarity', (1980) *Public Law* 367.

Erskine May: Parliamentary Practice (20th edn. 1983), Gordon, Sir C. (ed.), 'Questions to Ministers', pp. 331–47.

HUNT, Lord, of Tanworth, 'Access to a Previous Government's Papers', (1982) *Public Law* 514.

JENNINGS, Sir I., *Cabinet Government* (3rd edn. 1959), pp. 277–89.

MACKINTOSH, J., *The British Cabinet* (3rd edn. 1977).

MARSHALL, G., *Constitutional Conventions* (rev. edn., Oxford, 1986), pp. 54–61 and Appendix A.

NAYLOR, J. F., *Hankey, A Man and an Institution: The Cabinet Secretariat and the Custody of Cabinet Secrecy* (1984), chap. 7.

NORTON, P., 'Government Defeats in the House of Commons: Myth and Reality', (1978) *Public Law* 360.

OLIVER, D. and AUSTIN, R., 'Constitutional Aspects of the Westland Affair', (1987) *Parliamentary Affairs* 20.

RICHARDS, P. G., and RYLE, M., *Parliament Under Scrutiny* (forthcoming).

SILKIN, A., 'The Agreement to Differ of 1975 and its Effect on Ministerial Responsibility', (1977) *Political Quarterly* 65.

INDIVIDUAL RESPONSIBILITY

BAKER, R. J. S., 'The Vehicle and General Affair and Ministerial Responsibility', (1972) *Political Quarterly* 43.

FINER, S. E., 'The Individual Responsibility of Ministers', (1956) *Public Administration* 377.

FRY, G. K., 'The Sachsenhausen Case and the Convention of Ministerial Responsibility', (1970) *Public Law* 336.

MARSHALL, G., *Constitutional Conventions* (rev. edn., Oxford, 1986), pp. 61–6, 222–4.

NICOLSON, I. F. *The Mystery of Crichel Down* (1986).

Report of the Treasury and Civil Service Committee (Civil Servants and Ministers: Duties and Responsibilities) and Minutes of Evidence, HC 92; HC 92-i-viii (1985–6).

ROBINSON, A., SHEPHERD, R., RIDLEY, F. F., and JONES, G. W., 'Symposium on Ministerial Responsibility', (1987) *Public Administration* 61.

WHEARE, Sir K., *Maladministration and its Remedies* (1973), chap. 3.

—— 'Crichel Down Revisited', (1975) *Political Studies* 390.

MINISTERIAL RESPONSIBILITY GENERALLY

BARKER, A. (ed.), *Quangos in Britain* (1982).

BUTLER, D. E., 'Ministerial Responsibility in Australia and Britain', (1973) *Parliamentary Affairs* 26.

EDWARDS, J. Ll. J., *The Attorney-General, Politics, and the Public Interest* (1984).

FRY, G. K., 'Thoughts on the Recent State of the Convention of Ministerial Responsibility', (1969–70) *Parliamentary Affairs* 10.

JUDGE, D., *Ministerial Responsibility: Life in the Strawman Yet*, Strathclyde Papers in Government and Politics No. 37 (1984).

LEWIS, N., 'Who Controls Quangos and the Nationalized Industries?', in J. Jowell and D. Oliver (edd.), *The Changing Constitution* (Oxford, 1985).

SMITH, B. L. R., and HAGUE, D. C. (edd.), *The Dilemma of Accountability in Modern Government* (1971).

TURPIN, C., 'Ministerial Responsibility: Myth or Reality?', in J. Jowell and D. Oliver (edd.), *The Changing Constitution* (Oxford, 1985).

INDEX

Index compiled by Peva Keane